CRISIS MANAGEMENT IN CATHOLIC SCHOOLS

Thomas M. Batsis, O. Carm.

National Catholic Educational Association
Washington, DC

ISBN #1-55833-140-9

Table of Contents

Acknowledgments

In writing this book, I was guided by the suggestions, rough-draft readings, comments, expert advice, and encouragement of many others. I owe each a personal debt of gratitude. To mention but a few: Carol Ann Crede, principal of Visitation Elementary School, Los Angeles, CA; Erika Swenson, my research assistant; Chief Mike Olson, Culver City (CA) Fire Department; Firefighter Tamara Harrison, Office of Disaster Preparedness, City of Los Angeles Fire Department; JoAnn Isken, principal of Jefferson Elementary School, Lennox (CA) School District; canon law expert Father Mike Moody, S.J., Loyola Marymount University; Dr. Brian Leung, School of Education, Loyola Marymount University; Sr. Mary Elizabeth Galt, B.V.M., associate superintendent of schools, Archdiocese of Los Angeles; and Pat Ellis, superintendent of operations, Chevron U.S.A. (El Segundo, CA). A special note of thanks goes to Father Charles Kurgan, O. Carm., who read the manuscript and offered many helpful suggestions. Last but not least, my thanks to Diane and Ed, whose grief can only be fathomed by those who have lost a child through death.

Foreword

Unfortunately, modern American society has allowed to be created situations that cause many innocent persons untold hardships. The acceptance of violence by many people as a legitimate way to solve problems, the availability of guns, and the high pressure that some people live under have resulted in students being held captive or indiscriminately murdered. The widespread use of drugs and the unbridled use of alcohol have led to the injury or death of young children crossing streets in front of schools. The disregard for the sacredness of each individual has encouraged people to abuse children physically, mentally, and psychologically. These are situations that some school children have experienced and, unfortunately, will experience unless major changes are made in American society.

Catholic schools are communities built on a common acceptance of the message and person of Jesus. Because of this faith, they are in a unique position to enable students, parents, and faculty to come together in time of crisis and give support and assistance to one another. How a school community deals with such a situation is a true test of how deep its sense of community is.

While the membership of NCEA hope and pray that students and faculty in Catholic schools are never subjected to the test of handling the above crises, a reading of the daily newspaper provides the reasons for schools to be prepared to handle such situations. With this motivation, the NCEA Department of Elementary Schools is pleased to present this publication, *Crisis Management in Catholic Schools*. Father Thomas Batsis of Loyola Marymount University in Los Angeles presents a detailed plan to help schools set up their crisis management teams and offers directions on how these teams could function. Numerous simulations are provided to allow faculties and school communities to act out how they would handle specific crises. The department offers this book to the membership of NCEA so that all schools can be better prepared for an unexpected tragedy.

The NCEA Department of Elementary Schools expresses its deep gratitude to Father Batsis for sharing his experiences with the wider community. It gratefully acknowledges Tara McCallum, editorial assistant for the NCEA Department of Elementary Schools, for her work in editing and proofreading the manuscript and final text, and Tia Gray, in the NCEA Communications Department, for her work in designing the format.

Mary Ann Governal, OSF, Ed.D.　　*Robert J. Kealey, Ed.D.*
President　　*Executive Director*

NCEA Department of Elementary Schools
Feast of the Nativity of Mary, 1994

Preface

One of the sad ironies of life is that something good or worthwhile often emerges from the most incredible tragedy. Maybe it comes from either our need to explain or in some way deal with an experience that has nearly overwhelmed us. Possibly it arises from the desire to find some speck of goodness or just a kernel of redeeming value in an otherwise heartbreaking event. Thus it was for me with the genesis of this book. The heart of what is found in the following pages lies in the death of a child, struck down and killed as he and his dad were bicycling on a beautiful August morning about a week before school was due to begin. This tragedy was compounded by the accident's occurring just a block from his school, at an intersection where many students cross each day on their way to school.

I was one of the people called upon to help the school come to grips with the effects of that death on the child's classmates and on the school community. While I had an abundance of knowledge about how to deal with crises, and had experience helping others through periods of grief following the death of loved ones, this was the first time that I had assisted a school in working through the extended period of grief so necessary if healing was to take place.

Out of these events came a series of reflections on and convictions about how Catholic schools can deal with crisis. I am convinced that Catholic schools have special tools and resources, in the wellspring of faith, that can assist them in dealing with crises, large and small. As my own thinking developed, I realized the need not for a book focused on the narrow topic of death, but for a broader reflection on how Catholic schools can deal with the multitude of emergencies they face during the course of a school year. A systematic and focused plan for dealing with what at times may appear to be the unimaginable can greatly benefit the children who attend Catholic schools, and thus help heal the school community.

While the following pages may be of general interest to a wide audience of people involved in Catholic schools, my major purpose is to address Catholic school principals. This book is written, therefore, from the perspective of someone who has been a Catholic school principal. I hope that it will serve as a resource for those administrators wishing to implement a school crisis management team.

I chose first to cover topics separately. Repetition of the same idea or discussion appears in later chapters. This was done on purpose, hoping the reader will find it more helpful first to see key concepts presented in isolation and later to integrate them into discussions where application is a guiding principle. I believe this format will be practical for helping principals to build a school crisis management team.

Chapter 1 presents an overview of crisis management and focuses on how this concept differs in Catholic schools from its implementation in public schools. Chapter 2 offers suggestions for developing a crisis management team within a school. Chapter 3 focuses on a systematic plan for assessing the level of crisis, involving the team in a process that allows them to develop a more intimate knowledge of the school site and buildings. Chapter 4 discusses team training and preparation for crisis response.

The role of the principal, in developing the team and in working with the team during an actual crisis, is the subject of Chapter 5. Classroom teachers are literally the frontline people who will be dealing with any crisis; therefore, suggestions for training and crisis management from the teacher's perspective are presented in Chapter 6. Chapter 7 considers how the faith dimension of our lives becomes a rich reservoir to be utilized during crisis management. A major part of the discussion focuses on how faith can help children deal with a crisis event.

Chapter 8 offers a series of suggestions and a rationale for incorporating mental health professionals in a coordinated crisis response program. The important roles that these outside resources play in a crisis sometimes can be underestimated. Parents, like their children, are discussed throughout the book, but Chapter 9 offers an in-depth discussion on parents and how they should be managed during a crisis.

Chapter 10 looks at the role played by the priest/pastor during a school-related emergency, with suggestions for incorporating the parish's spiritual leader into the crisis response. Finally, Chapter 11 offers a brief summary of the book and attempts to pull together and integrate the various elements of the previous chapters.

There are three appendices. First, an outline is provided for developing a school crisis team response manual. Next is an agenda for a day-long workshop for crisis teams. The third appendix offers a series of practice simulations to help team members work through problem situations.

An annotated list of suggested articles and books is included to offer additional resources to call upon as needed.

I hope this book leads you to action: to set up your own crisis management team and to share your experience with a neighboring principal. If you have any comments on this publication, I invite you to share them with me.

Tom M. Batsis, O. Carm.
Loyola Marymount University
Los Angeles, CA
February 1994

About the Author

Tom Batsis, O. Carm., is associate professor of education at Loyola Marymount University in Los Angeles, CA. He teaches courses in human development and counseling. Father Batsis has a master's degree in school administration and a doctorate clinical psychology. Prior to his faculty appointment at Loyola Marymount, he was a high school teacher, counselor, and administrator. A presenter at four previous NCEA conventions, he is frequently called upon as a consultant to Catholic elementary and secondary schools. In addition, he has a private practice as a psychologist. Currently Father Batsis is a member of the Los Angeles archdiocesan school board.

Chapter 1

Crisis Management and the Catholic School

A n unfortunate aspect of our lives as educators is that we have to deal with challenges that even twenty years ago would have been nearly unimaginable. Children bringing firearms onto campuses and adults entering school yards with the intent of killing children are two of the more dramatic illustrations of this new reality. While some may think of these examples as more applicable to large, inner-city public schools, we know that such heinous acts occur even in the unlikely settings of rural parish elementary schools.

Many emergencies occur each day in schools throughout the country. Crisis situations can range from a child falling and being injured on the playground, to slanderous rumors being circulated about a teacher, to a criminally insane madman entering a school building, intent on harming children. In each case, school officials have to make a response that is primarily focused on insuring the safety of students and staff, admittedly no easy task.

Because crisis situations rarely come at opportune times, school officials may find themselves dazed, confused, and wondering what to do next when faced with an emergency. While a sense of disorientation is a normal response to an emergency, school officials who have properly planned for just such a contingency are in a much better position to respond in an appropriate and sensitive way.

Although it may not be possible to anticipate the multitude of crises that may occur in a school, administrators, faculty, and staff can assess the ability of a school to respond to emergencies. This assessment has two goals: first, to examine the school closely to see whether there are dangers present that practically invite an emergency to take place and second, to develop a plan for response once an emergency has occurred.

Crisis Defined

What is a crisis? A crisis is any event that brings the ongoing schedule of activities to a standstill. A crisis, by its very nature, causes chaos that is seemingly not containable. A temporary disruption in the school schedule by an event that at first appears to be a crisis may, within a brief period of time, be resolved, with schedules and routines returning to normal. For example, two students fighting in the cafeteria may disrupt the lunch period and cause some havoc, but the problem can quickly be resolved and the cafeteria schedule returned to normal once the two combatants are separated and sent to the office. This probably would not be considered a crisis, because the event was not totally unmanageable and was able to be contained.

What constitutes a crisis, therefore, seems to depend on a number of variables. What makes for a crisis in one school might not necessarily have the same effect in another school. Some people and certain schools just seem better able to adjust to interruptions than others. This point will be discussed in greater detail in the following chapter.

As obvious as all this may seem, these are the reasons why it is so imperative that each school defines in general terms what constitutes a crisis. This should be followed by taking preventive steps, by planning and preparing ways to cope with disruptions that might affect the physical, psychological, and spiritual well-being of the entire school. For example, if two groups of ethnically different students become aggressive and hostile in the cafeteria, matters could very quickly escalate to the point where the student body is polarized, parents are involved out of concern for their children's safety, and the entire school day is aborted. This situation could very easily become unmanageable and unrestrained. School officials would need to respond quickly, yet with cautious sensitivity, to resolve a situation that could disrupt the educational process and affect school climate for an undetermined amount of time.

Many school principals would say that their days as an administrator are filled with crises, large and small. Spending a day in a principal's office would convince anyone of this statement's validity. Although some schools seem to have more than their share of events that could be termed crises, it takes only one real emergency to show an administrator just how unprepared the school is for such an eventuality. Many events that might be termed emergencies can usually be managed within a relatively short time, with the school returning soon to its normal functions. On the other hand, a true crisis can turn a school to near chaos, leaving administrators panicking as they scramble to identify (1) the nature of the event, (2) the seriousness of the event, (3) an appropriate level of response, and (4) the available resources to aid in the response.

Unfortunately, because of the very nature of an emergency, the four steps identified above must be carried out almost simultaneously and with what may appear to be breakneck speed. On the other hand, experience with phoned-in bomb scares, for instance, alerts us to the need also for caution, so major mistakes that leave school officials vulnerable to a charge of having acted precipitously or in a totally inappropriate manner will not be made.

The foregoing speaks to the need for advanced planning. Yet, frequently there is a desire to put off such work, as if doing it would be to engage in a morbid act. No one enjoys thinking about problems, especially serious ones, and certainly no one relishes the thought of preparing for situations that could develop into crises. Statistics, however, don't present an optimistic picture. For example, in just one school year, one in six students in public and in private schools reports witnessing either a threat of an attack or an actual attack upon a teacher, and 15 percent of all students report the presence of street gangs in their schools (Alsalam, Ogle, Rogers, & Smith, 1992). Estimates are that over 270,000 students carry weapons to school each day ("Youth Violence," 1993) and three million crimes are committed on school grounds each year (Harper, 1989). Violence is but one type of emergency that can test the resources of a school. Thus, it is not being overly dramatic to state that it is not a matter of whether a crisis will strike a school, but when it will come.

Advanced planning should be preventive and provide a positive approach to responding to threatening situations. The school that has carefully thought through a response to crisis may not be able to anticipate every possibility, but it will be in a better position to respond to unforeseen events than the school that continues to deny the need for planning, only to find itself later facing a dire emergency.

Some people also argue that crises, by their nature, are so unusual that planning is futile. After all, so the logic of this argument goes, crises are by definition events so out of the ordinary that one cannot anticipate the best level of response. This argument would probably hold up if we were to examine disaster response only on a superficial level. When we look more closely at agencies responsible for responding to emergencies, however, we readily see these organizations expending a lot of time and resources on anticipating disasters. A recent tour of a local fire department's central station provided an enlightening example. The conference room walls were covered with charts and notes from a recent disaster-response drill. A cursory examination of the charts revealed an attempt to consider the greatest number of possibilities. It appeared the team had focused on answering questions that began with two words: "What if...?"

Fire departments, of course, are trained in disaster response and exist for that purpose. Schools, it can be argued, do not exist to handle disaster. Nevertheless, when you bring together many people who work, learn, play, and eat together each day in a school, plus take into account their ages, you have a setting primed for an emergency. This is all the more reason to plan thoughtfully for such a possibility.

One final argument to support crisis planning comes from law. An unfortunate aspect of modern life is that we live in what some would claim is a very litigious society, where "I'll sue you" is a threat heard with increasing frequency. Thus, we can be sure that not planning in some meaningful way for a crisis might well open school authorities to a charge of having acted in a negligent manner by failing to anticipate the possibility of crisis.

Public school educators have done a very good job of documenting responses to crises. In fact, a lot of the literature on crisis management is written from that perspective and invariably makes reference to the resources a school district supplied. When a public school faces an emergency that requires a response by psychologists, for example, most districts are able to utilize central office psychologists and neighboring school counselors to aid the affected school. This level of response to crises stands in sharp contrast to that of most Catholic schools. While there may be a central office serving the diocesan schools, that office is usually staffed by only a few personnel, who hardly command the resources available to a public school district office. This is a reality we have to deal with, a consideration lacking in most of the articles and books on the subject.

While we may envy the resources a public school has in responding to a crisis, there is one critical resource we have to call upon that is not directly available to public educational systems. The ability to express our faith and to openly call upon it in time of need is a valuable tool we have in dealing with crises. This resource and the appropriate manner for utilizing religious faith in times of crisis will be discussed at length in Chapter 7. The premise here is that expressing our religious experience is a critical dimension of the Catholic school's and the individual's ability to deal with crisis.

Summary

An awareness of the increasing levels of violence in our society is the basis for establishing a school crisis management team. This chapter discussed possible characteristics of crises and a rationale for attempting to manage emergencies. Stress was placed on the concept that crises can be managed, and an overview on developing a crisis response team was presented.

Chapter 2

Developing a Crisis Management Team

Choosing and training a crisis management team requires a good deal of thought, planning, and effort. Several questions need to be considered in advance, and among them are (1) How will a team function in the school? (2) Who is available and willing to work on the team? (3) Who is most appropriate for the team, in terms of their ability to work in a team environment and under what, at times, will be extreme pressure? (4) What resources are needed and available to establish a team? Seeking answers to all of these questions in advance will help you make the best choices in setting up a crisis management team.

This chapter is divided into three sections. The first focuses on working through some basic questions and choices that need to be made in setting up a crisis management team for a school. The second section deals with selecting team members and initial training for the team. Finally, there is a discussion of ongoing training and work with team members.

Background Questions and Issues

Planning is the key element in establishing an effective crisis management team. As with other areas of the school's operation, there is no substitute for thoughtful, thorough planning when it comes to crisis management. Working through the initial questions and needs for a team will help avoid serious missteps in the later development and work of a team. Nothing could be more embarrassing or more disheartening to team morale than for the team to find out some months after it had begun work that a whole series of regulations exist governing how it should function. Since this chapter focuses on critical questions and issues that need to be resolved in establishing a team, it might be very helpful to keep a notebook and pen handy and to frequently utilize a brainstorming method to work through questions and ideas as they arise. During the creative process, some of our best ideas come when we leave a problem and move on to something else. Providing opportunities to brainstorm about this paramount issue in school management may have beneficial results.

Since each school is unique, examples and topics presented in this chapter may not be relevant to every situation. Principals, aware of their schools' unique characteristics and special needs, are best able to determine when to adopt, when to adapt, and when to forget the suggestions made by others.

Relationship to a central schools office. The first question that needs to be answered concerns the relationship between the school and the larger administrative body. Public schools, being directly governed by administrative regulations from the central board of education, have little flexibility in this area. The board usually provides strong guidance and supervisory personnel to individual schools to resolve the many issues that arise. As the reader's experience no doubt confirms, Catholic schools have a very different administrative structure, and frequently individual schools operate with a lot of independence within a loosely defined structure. The principal, therefore, needs to discover what information is available from the central diocesan office. This will help to determine the degree of freedom to exercise in setting up the team.

Several questions will help move the process forward: Is there a diocesan handbook for school administrators with a section on handling emergencies? If there are regulations on this topic, what parameters do they set for the work of a crisis management team in a school? If there are no written regulations, does the central office have any expectations regarding the development of a school crisis management team? Are there any resources available from the central schools office to aid individual schools faced with a crisis? Does that office provide training for a crisis team? If it is a parish school, how much independence does the principal have in setting up a crisis team? What role has the pastor taken regarding school policy? If the school is staffed by a religious order, has a working group developed policies for creating a team?

How the Team Will Work

A very important issue is how the principal conceptualizes the work of a crisis management team. One way to help you decide what constitutes the work of such a team is to read this book. Another way to resolve this issue is to gather more information by visiting other schools and talking with other administrators. A good question to ask is, What would you change, given another opportunity to establish a school crisis management team? Asking principals what they learned and what mistakes have been made in setting up a team may provoke a refreshingly honest response. Most principals will be willing to offer very candid assessments of errors to avoid.

While a wise administrator is open to the ideas and experiences of others, it is important to view matters with a critical eye. Caution in adopting a program is necessary because what works so well in one school may prove disastrous in another. Exercising caution in noting these differences before borrowing ideas or plans from others will result in time well spent. Illustrating this point, one parish elementary school may have a team that works extremely well because of the pastor's active involvement and support. He understands the need for a crisis management team and has supported the establishment of such a team by participating in team training and meetings, as needed. Or, there may be a parish administrator who is at best benign regarding the school's very existence and certainly does not welcome any involvement in crisis management team training. Or, again, the pastor may be supportive but just does not have the time for or interest in being an active team member. Working through and resolving these issues in advance will help the principal to decide what is best for the school's particular situation.

Definition of emergencies. Another crucial issue is how the team will function in response to emergencies in the school. How are emergencies defined? Will a team be brought together frequently to assist in responding to large and small crises during the school year, or will the team function only when a crisis of a very unusual nature occurs, leaving the other emergencies to be handled by administrators?

Deciding in advance how the team will function will greatly affect the type of training that will be implemented once the team has been assembled. Having team members work together on a series of problems during the school year is probably a good way to keep them ready for response to a bigger crisis. On the other hand, having the team work on many emergencies may become cumbersome, time-consuming, and plainly inefficient. Possibly, the team may end up working on problems that might easily be handled and resolved in the main office. Furthermore, once the team's role is defined in a broad sense, it may become very difficult to restrict its scope of responsibility. So, deciding in advance just how the team will function and determining the scope of its responsibility are questions needing resolution early in the planning process.

Team composition and size. Team composition and size are usually determined by the type of school and size of the student body. For example, in a high school, which usually has an administrative staff, the principal may choose team members from among that group, supplementing with someone from among the teaching staff. In a small elementary school, however, the need may be to rely on teachers and even outside resource personnel for the team. An obvious team member would be the school counselor, who could become crucial as an advisor and in working through trauma witnessed by students. Utilizing resources from outside the school staff may be an option the team wishes to discuss.

Regarding size, the task is to keep a balance between the extreme of a team so large that it is unable to function efficiently and a group so small that it becomes overwhelmed in responding to the many tasks that arise in a crisis response. Attempting to conceptualize how the team will function in the particular school, what tasks it might encounter, and then beginning to picture the number of people who will form the school's team may prove helpful while reading the following pages. This is one way to determine team size for the school.

Team chemistry. Team members will have to function

together under the most difficult circumstances. In most schools teachers are quite comfortable functioning in a nearly autonomous fashion, having become masters of their own kingdoms—their classrooms. The opportunity to make independent decisions within the broader confines of school policy is something that most teachers would welcome. By contrast, crisis management will require a team effort, with people having to work together in a pressure-cooker atmosphere and to arrive at mutually agreed-upon decisions. Also, while decisions at times will come down to the principal, as team leader, team members will need to understand that there is no room for disagreement once a decision has been made. A team member publicly disagreeing with a decision about how best to handle a crisis, for instance, would completely undermine the team's ability to function effectively. Team members, therefore, should be chosen for their ability to work together and their willingness to continue working with a decision they may not completely accept.

Initial meeting. After deciding on team membership, the next task will be to decide whether to meet with the individuals separately or to call everyone together as a group. This decision probably will be based on personal leadership style, since some administrators feel more comfortable in a one-on-one situation when asking people to be part of a project, while others feel that a group situation might provide the best atmosphere. However one chooses to proceed, it is best to decide this prior to any announcement concerning a school crisis management team.

The initial meeting with team members will focus on covering basic issues, such as the reasons why a crisis management team is being formed, the reasons why individual team members have been chosen (what skills, qualities, and areas of representation they bring to the group), how the team will function, and the team's scope of responsibility. Resolving these issues before holding any meetings with team members or making an announcement to the general school community will help reinforce the perception of the principal acting in the best interests of the entire school community.

The meeting with team members will focus on answering as fully as possible questions about the purpose and function of a crisis management team. After all, no team has been functioning at this particular school site and allowing the team to evolve in its unique manner can greatly reinforce its competence. It is also important, however, to keep two goals in mind. First is clarifying the team's role. The group will not be some form of a school management team. In general, the principal will decide which problem/issue constitutes a crisis for the team's input and will be the ultimate decision-maker in a crisis. Second is eliciting from individuals a commitment to serve as team members. Once a team has been chosen, a general announcement can be made to the school community.

Team training. A question to settle before any training is whether to hire a consultant from outside the school. To do so would involve using financial resources that might be needed in other areas of school operation. An advantage, however, is that a consultant would bring expertise to training sessions that will, hopefully, make the most economical use of the team's time. Trainers can be drawn from a local college or university that offers courses in crisis management, a public school district that forms crisis management teams for its schools, or a nearby Catholic school that has a team that functions well. The trainer usually works with the team on a periodic basis, over several months. Additional trainers can be brought in from mental health centers, emergency medical services (EMS), and the police and fire departments.

Neighboring schools also may be interested in forming a crisis response team. Thus, the cost of bringing in a consultant to help initiate the training process could be shared among several schools. Since the beginning steps in forming a crisis team are specific to each school's situation, the contributing schools would not end up being locked into the same type of team. Another advantage is that working with three or four other schools, each with its own team of four or five people, would help to increase the flow and exchange of ideas. This is particularly true when compiling a list of community resources for the disaster response manual.

In implementing team training, there are many community resources that may be used for assistance. Three of them are the fire department/paramedics, the police department, and the Red Cross. Each of these groups functions in a particular way when focusing on an aspect of crisis response and can be very helpful with team training. Asking each of these groups to assist with training, especially in a situation where several schools are cooperating, is the type of community service these agencies welcome.

Initial training. Team training during the first stage focuses on gathering resources and assessing the school site. Team members might either be assigned or volunteer for tasks that will accomplish these goals. Once these two goals have been met, the team can review its findings and compile a document that forms the core of its emergency response manual. Each member gets a copy of this manual.

Development of an emergency response manual. The development of the school's emergency response manual is a critical, first training function for the team because this manual will serve as the major resource utilized during an emergency. It is important, therefore, that team members be actively involved in planning the manual and gathering information that will become the essential elements of this guide. Nothing can be more detrimental to the team's functioning than for the members to use a preassembled book, one that has already been developed by the principal or some other person on the team. Their personal involvement will aid the members' knowledge about crisis response and increase team effectiveness in responding to an actual emergency.

Needs of the school. While a strong argument has been presented for the team to develop its own resource guide, there are questions and issues that can point the team toward gathering useful information to be placed in the school's emergency response book. A series of such questions is presented in the section on surveying the school's environment in Chapter 3. These questions prompt the team as it begins to develop a statement about the unique characteristics of the school site and neighboring area. This statement should be a bricf but comprehensive narrative presenting a picture of the school. Questions will emerge from this statement which the team will need to address in providing for an adequate response to crisis.

Chapter 4 contains a list of resources the school can call upon in responding to a crisis. This list ranges from the location and telephone number of the local emergency medical response team to the telephone number of the local power company. Information and resource needs will develop as team members begin asking what-if questions.

Second Training Phase

After gathering the data that form the core of information in the crisis guide, the team will develop a training plan. This training should focus on fine-tuning the team's ability to respond in an effective manner to a crisis; therefore, the team will need to practice a series of hypothetical scenarios. Here is where employing the services of an outside trainer or consultant might be considered, to provide meaningful and critical feedback that the team can use to increase its effectiveness.

This second phase of training might be an excellent time to call upon other principals and teams to ask them to reflect on how their teams handled an actual emergency. Most principals and teams are quite willing to share their experiences and help others learn from the things they did right and from any mistakes that were made. In a session of this nature, it is always important to note common characteristics shared with another team/school and any significant differences.

Frequently, police departments and other public service agencies are willing to provide training to school personnel. What will add leverage to such a request is having teams from five or six neighboring schools participate in this training, thus giving the agency access to a large group. Large-group workshops also have the added advantage of providing opportunities for cross-fertilization of ideas.

Final training. Training never has a final phase, in terms of there being an end point; rather, it is a matter of reaching that stage where the principal has set up a team and then moving into a maintenance mode, where team members remain prepared to respond to a crisis. What is important in this phase is to avoid thinking that once initial training has been completed, the team will be able to respond to an emergency at some point. Recognizing the value of ongoing training to maintain an optimal level of readiness for response is the key to a successful crisis response team. Schools can get into serious trouble when they have developed a plan for responding to a particular problem, practiced it through some form of drill, but set it aside to gather dust. When faced with an actual emergency, such schools experience pandemonium as everyone scrambles, trying to remember what to do.

Review of the manual. In general, the emergency response manual will include the team's purpose and how it functions in a crisis, plans for responding to various emergencies, and resources that can be contacted for assistance. After the manual is in its last-draft form, copies should be given to a small group of key people for review and suggestions. These people might include the pastor, the area coordinator/supervisor, a principal from a neighboring school, and a parent. They should be asked to read it with a critical eye, writing notes on the pages and responding to the questions, "What has been left out?" "What has the team failed to anticipate?"

Once this group has reviewed the manual, the team will need to consider the reviewers' recommendations and decide whether to include them in the final draft. A copy of the manual should be kept in computerized form for updating as needed.

Summary

A school's ability to handle an emergency will depend primarily on the quality of its crisis management team. This chapter explored the rationale for establishing such a team; the process for forming the team, including the issues to consider in choosing team members; the phases of training; putting together an emergency response manual; and resources to call upon to help with team training. Practical suggestions were offered for carrying out this process.

Chapter 3

Crisis Assessment

Crises can be broadly categorized as originating from either a natural disaster or human error. Examples of crises from natural disasters are tornados and earthquakes. Natural disasters can damage buildings and injure or kill people, and there is little anyone can do to prevent them. The other type of crisis originates from human failure or malice. An explosion resulting from poorly monitored chemicals in a science classroom is an example of this type of disaster. This is clearly a crisis that may have been averted with timely inspections and inventorying of supplies.

This chapter focuses on preventing crises through timely and thorough monitoring of the school site.* In implementing the strategies suggested here, an administrator or crisis management team may be able to minimize the effects of some emergencies that cannot be avoided. This assessment is best carried out by a team of two or three school personnel, rather than by just a single administrator.

Building and Grounds

Neighboring areas. Begin outside the building. Walk the property and closely examine the school site. Are busy streets and thoroughfares near the school? Is a business district nearby? Do any of these businesses have customers who, by the nature of the business, might pose a threat to children? Bars, liquor stores, and pornographic bookstores are examples of businesses that might have such customers. Are large manufacturing plants, chemical plants, or hazardous material disposal sites nearby?

---

*Watson, R. S., Poda, J. H., Miller, C. T., Rice, E. S., & West, G., 1990, was an excellent resource for this chapter.

Do any of these pose potential dangers for students, or would explosions/fires from these places endanger students while they are at school? An affirmative response to any of these questions indicates the need to deal with these external threats to students.

While conducting this external assessment of the area immediately adjacent to the school, locate the nearest fire station, police station, and emergency medical response unit. Note how emergency equipment can arrive at the school. How would emergency equipment enter the property? Is there easy access for emergency medical response units to the school yard? Would gates need to be unlocked or barriers removed? If so, who controls keys and has responsibility for removing barriers? Are barriers locked into the ground?

Perimeter of the school grounds. Next consider the school property itself. Walking the perimeter of the grounds and looking at how the school buildings are situated on the property may prove enlightening. Architectural drawings of the site should be examined closely. If no such plans exist, drawings should be made of the school site because they could be extremely helpful to police and fire officials in an emergency.

Examine the boundaries of the school property. Is fencing properly maintained? If there is no fencing of the school yard, what prevents an unwelcome visitor from entering the grounds? Some schools plant shrubbery in front of the fence. While this may look attractive, it also provides a hiding place for someone planning to attack children on the playground or kidnap a youngster walking to or from school. Consider either removing or trimming back plants that are large and obscure your line of sight on and off the property.

School yard entrances/exits. Are barriers in place at the entrances to the school yard while classes are in session? Consider locking gates and preventing easy access to the playground areas of the school. If this is not possible or if there are no gates present to block someone walking onto the property, consider placing barriers that would prevent a vehicle from entering the property without someone first having to stop and remove them. Supervision of the school yard/playground area is discussed later in this chapter in the section about on-campus communications.

Playground and recess areas. While surveying the playground and general school yard areas of the property, observe whether the grounds are properly maintained. Is play equipment safe and kept in generally good repair? If it has become worn, does it pose potential danger to students, who could be cut or seriously injured?

All trash and disposal sites should be away from playground areas and should not be readily accessible to children, particularly those in the lower grades. Has trash or cast-off supplies been allowed to accumulate in areas where children might be injured if they were playing in the vicinity? Are trash disposal bins properly secured and fenced, making them inaccessible to students who might crawl into them without being seen by playground supervisory staff?

Look for obstructions or pipes that may be sticking out of the ground in such a way that they might go unnoticed and possibly injure children who did not see them. Are necessary obstructions (e.g., pipes for ground watering) properly marked with a bright color to prevent someone tripping over one hidden from sight?

Building exteriors. Now focus on exterior portions of buildings. If children and teachers had to exit through windows, would this be relatively easy? Windows should be considered emergency exits in case doors are blocked. If there are two or more floors to the classroom buildings, could firefighters easily place ladders up against the building?

Back to plants and shrubbery. In addition to removing bushes and shrubbery or at least keeping them well trimmed so they do not provide a hiding place for an intruder, it is important to keep trees on the property properly maintained. Are there dead branches on trees that might continue to rot and eventually fall on someone passing nearby?

Building entrances. Are doors in good working order, allowing easy exit from the building in case of emergency? Are some doors kept locked during the school day to prevent entrance by unauthorized persons? While a door may not be locked to prevent someone from exiting the building during normal school hours, since this would clearly violate the law, consider locking entrances to deter unmonitored building access. This is especially important for doors located away from the office area. Due to safety concerns, however, entrances adjacent to the playground area should never be locked when children are outside because an emergency outside could make it necessary to bring children quickly into the building. Examples would be someone off the property firing a weapon at children on the playground or the threat of an earthquake or electrical storm.

Entryway and visitor policy. Is the main entryway to the building monitored throughout the school day? Are visitors routed to the main office for clearance to gain access to classrooms and other areas? If not, a procedure should be instituted for handling visitors. For example, all visitors could be required to wear some identification symbol they obtain at the office and return there at the conclusion of their business. Anyone not wearing a visitor's badge outside the office area would then be conspicuous. Children are frequently the first to note the presence of a stranger. It is important that they understand the visitor policy and that they are instructed to inform teachers or staff if they see a stranger not wearing a visitor's identification.

An objection to this procedure might be that a major attraction of Catholic schools is the frequency of parental visits, and requiring visitor badges might offend parents or deter their visits. When policies are explained, especially this one, as being for the protection of the students, however, most reasonable adults willingly comply and within a relatively short time everyone thinks the procedure has always been the policy.

Hallways and stairwells. Are hallways and stairwells properly lit during the school day? Are there any obstructions in hallways that might pose a danger to students and staff attempting to make a quick exit from the building during an emergency? Are stairwells properly maintained? Are steps and handrails anchored securely? Are lighting fixtures properly maintained and well anchored to the ceiling or wall? Is there some form of emergency lighting in case of a power loss? Are there glass display cases, lockers that are not flat against the wall, or other types of fixtures that stick out in such a way that children might be injured while attempting to escape from the building? Such potential dangers need attention.

Emergency signaling equipment. Most schools have emergency alarms, fire extinguishers, and/or fire hoses in hallways. These need to be examined regularly to insure proper maintenance. When was the last time fire extinguishers were checked? Is there a regular schedule for refilling extinguishers? The alarm system is usually tested from the control panel in the main office, however, it should be tested at least once each year from the stations located in hallways, where the signal will most likely originate in an emergency.

Classrooms. In an emergency requiring a speedy exit from classrooms, the two logical routes are through doors and windows. Is there more than one door providing access to and egress from classrooms? If not, do windows open enough to allow students and adults to exit through them? If they do not, can a window in each room be enlarged to allow for emergency exit? Windows may often be overlooked as a means of escape from classrooms.

Classroom doors should contain windows large enough for easy viewing from the hallway into the room and vice versa. Check to make sure windows are not blocked or obscured in any way. Can teachers lock classroom doors from the inside in an emergency? An example of when this would be necessary is when an intruder has entered the building and teachers are alerted through coded messages over the public-address or classroom telephone system to this potential threat to safety. Being able to lock classrooms quickly without having to open doors and enter the hallway could save valuable seconds and many lives.

Within the classroom, make a visual inspection to locate potential hazards. Lighting fixtures should be tested to make sure they are properly anchored to ceilings or walls. Are there electrical cords or exposed wiring that might endanger students? Are tables, chairs, and desks in good condition? Are large pieces of equipment anchored to keep them from falling on students during a natural emergency, such as an earthquake or tornado? Are there obstructions in the classroom that would block easy exit from the room?

Communications Systems

A thorough assessment of communications devices and systems will prove essential in a crisis. For this discussion, communications are divided into those devices that serve to help the school communicate with the surrounding community and equipment that facilitates communication on the campus.

Telephones. Usually the telephones in school offices are considered sufficient to alert community authorities to an emergency on campus. It is quite possible, however, that telephone lines may be tied up during an emergency with incoming calls of concern. Consider having an unlisted number to use to alert authorities and to serve as an open line of communication between emergency personnel and school officials. The best location for this phone is probably in the principal's office.

Since telephones are electrical devices, they generally operate from the local power source. During an interruption in electrical service, phones may be used to dial out but the signal for an incoming call may not be functioning due to power failure.

Furthermore, the crisis may be of such magnitude that all telephone service is cut; therefore, consider locating a citizens band (CB) radio or similar device in the office area. This may become your only link to fire, police, and other local and governmental agencies. Before purchasing such a device, ask if a parent or someone else in the community can donate this equipment to the school. It is also a good idea to have a member of the office staff trained to use it.

On-campus communications. The usual means of communication between administrative offices and classrooms is a public-address system. The older systems allow only for communication that is initiated by the office to individual rooms or to the entire campus. There needs to be some means to allow a teacher to signal the office that an emergency exists in the classroom. Also, consider having in each room telephone-type handsets that allow a teacher to communicate privately with the office, and vice versa, about matters that would disturb students. Additionally, teachers might be given a code word they could use to signal that conditions in the classroom are normal and one to signal that an emergency exists.

Communication between the playground and office is absolutely essential but, unfortunately, often overlooked. When students are outside the building and under staff supervision, someone needs to have access to a handheld communications device. Commonly referred to as a walkie-talkie, this device can save valuable time and lives during an emergency. It can be purchased in a variety of stores and is now moderately priced. A school bake sale or a generous benefactor could easily provide the funds to purchase such a device.

It might be beneficial for all administrators to carry a walkie-talkie while moving throughout the campus. The ability to signal others and to be informed about an emergency can save precious time during the first minutes of a crisis, when time is critical.

School Records

Information filed on each student and staff member is a key resource in an emergency, so it is essential that records be kept current and accurate. Today's increasing technological sophistication directly impacts the expanded use of computers for storing and retrieving information. This technology is extremely helpful in the day-to-day operation of a school and in providing information quickly on students in a crisis situation. If the school has a power loss, however, retrieval of computer-stored records would be impossible. The school, therefore, needs to maintain accurate hard-copy information for the crisis team to use.

Each student record should include basic information, such as name and telephone number of a person to contact, plus names of persons to whom the child may be released in an emergency. Consider updating this information on a biannual basis. If both parents are living in the home, or if there is joint custody, the record should indicate where each parent can be contacted during the day. If both parents work, the telephone number at each parent's work site should be part of the student's school record.

Medical information may prove essential in an emergency, especially notations about a child's potential for allergic reaction to any medication and the need for regular medication during the day. To easily identify students who are allergic to certain medications, a flagging system can be used that involves placing bright-colored dots at a convenient place on the record (bright-colored marking pens serve the same purpose). School administrators might consider using this flagging system for a variety of other purposes. Children who are victims of an acrimonious divorce, for example, are at an increased risk of reactions that involve self-inflicted injury and an increased risk of being abducted by one parent. When such a situation becomes known, the student's record could be identified, a move that may be invaluable and critically time-saving when dealing with a crisis involving such a child. Finally, it is important to include a current picture of the student as part of his or her record.

Computers

This technology has the advantage of allowing nearly instantaneous information retrieval, as opposed to searching through numerous files. Having computer files stored with access possible through a variety of variables allows a crisis management team to retrieve information in multiple ways. The best way to achieve this capability is to hire someone who knows programming and can help address your particular needs. Often a student from a nearby college or university can provide invaluable and cost-effective assistance with this task.

Summary

The responsible and professional approach to preventing or minimizing the effects of a crisis is to address concerns well in advance of any emergency. This chapter focused on possible ways to accomplish this task. By working at becoming knowledgeable about the building, grounds, and important school systems, administrators and team members may avert some crises and mitigate the impact of other emergencies through careful advance planning. Thinking through the specific and unique needs of the school and identifying important tools and resources that the team may need to use to respond to a potential or imminent crisis will increase the team's overall sense of purpose and importance and will ultimately help it to deal more effectively with the danger at hand.

Crisis Response: A Plan for Action

As has been pointed out, an emergency can turn a smoothly functioning school into a chaotic maelstrom, with administrators scrambling to identify (1) the nature of the event, (2) the seriousness of the event, (3) an appropriate level of response, and (4) the available resources to aid that response. The purpose of a crisis management team is to stop further deterioration and contain the situation in order to return the school to normal functioning. Depending upon the crisis, this intervention may last for a few hours, a few weeks, or, in some cases, several months.

This chapter focuses on how a team works to develop responses to crises. In particular, the four points listed above are developed to demonstrate how a team functions in a crisis response.

Team Response

A team will be more efficient in its work and more effective in its response if it follows a preestablished plan for working together. In the following paragraphs, a four-step plan is suggested for resolving emergencies (for additional suggestions, see Leung, 1993). These four steps will be easier to implement if the team has practiced a response with hypothetical situations (see Appendix C), later going back to question how a different response might be more effective.

Identifying the nature of the event. The first few minutes or hours, depending on what has occurred, are critical in the crisis team's response to an emergency. This time is spent gathering information that answers three basic questions: (1) What has happened? (2) Who was involved? and (3) Are there injuries or deaths? Often the first question is easier to answer than the remaining two. Regardless, it is vital to gather accurate information on what has occurred.

It is important for team members to come together in some predetermined location, in a place where conversations can take place in private and confidentiality can be assured. While school personnel will need to communicate with the crisis team, feeding appropriate information and seeking instructions on how to proceed, there is a need also to insure the team's privacy in order to provide an atmosphere for open communication among team members. At times it may not be possible to gather in the place designated as the crisis team's work area and an alternate location will have to be used. For example, the emergency might be an earthquake that destroys part or all of the school building, making it impossible for the team to work out of the school's conference room and necessitating the team's move to a predetermined space in the parish center. Selecting several alternate sites can be one of the training activities for team members.

Just as the team functions best under the guidance of a designated leader, so also team efficiency will improve if other key roles are quickly assigned. While other roles may unfold, depending largely upon the nature of the crisis, the recorder is a key role that can be assigned in advance. The recorder's function may appear insignificant, but when the team is at a critical juncture in handling the emergency, invariably someone will ask about information gathered earlier. Assigning a team member to keep an accurate record of information, therefore, can be extremely helpful.

This record should begin with the complete date and specific time that the team came together. Notes on the team's work can be kept in a notebook, or, preferably, in a combination of written notes and wall charts or chalkboard notes. Using wall charts helps everyone gain a better picture as events unfold. If conditions permit, a computer-driven word-processing program would be very helpful in assisting the team's recordkeeping.

This record will prove helpful basically in two instances. First, the team may well benefit from reviewing the manner in which it addressed events surrounding the crisis by seeing where improvements can be made in its response to a future emergency. Second, a parent or group of parents may later question the appropriateness of the team's response, and a written record can be helpful in addressing these concerns. This written record can be helpful also if a negligence suit is brought against the school.

Assessing seriousness. Accuracy in assessing the seriousness of the event is crucial and depends on the information that has been gathered. This assessment may require at times a greater level of expertise than is available among the team members, however, and they will need to recognize this fact and determine whether to use outside expertise for help. Do others possess special knowledge or a perspective that will aid the team's work, or would the inclusion of others merely complicate matters? Only the team can make this determination. Because a true crisis involves the physical, psychological, and/or spiritual well-being of people, nothing should be dismissed as unimportant until it is assessed and evaluated. Sometimes the team must make a quick judgment call. Hopefully, they will be prepared for such emergencies through their training.

Responding appropriately and effectively. An appropriate level of response to an emergency requires a lot of wisdom and common sense. In all instances, the team should avoid overreacting, but it also should be careful to avoid creating the perception that it has failed to acknowledge the seriousness of a crisis. Put simply, the team needs to answer the question, "What do we need to do to resolve this situation?"

In a school environment, there is always the danger of a reaction to a crisis that does little more than increase the level of anxiety and panic among children, thus leading to the possibility of even more injury, both physical and psychological. Effective teachers and administrators, therefore, always work at keeping a sense of outward calm in such situations, even though they may be experiencing a good measure of inner panic. Yet, there are times when the need is to act quickly and decisively for the protection of the students. If a sociopath takes out a gun and begins shooting randomly at children on the playground, for example, an appropriate response is to quickly shout orders to take cover and/or run for the building.

An appropriate level of response must take into account the perception of how the school is handling the crisis. It is important to maintain a sense of control and containment while acting in a manner that reassures parents the school is serious about responding to a perceived threat to the safety of their children.

As an example, plans in a crisis response manual need to include a procedure for locking down the campus in certain emergency situations. This would mean locking all outside doors and access gates to the campus to protect the safety of the children and staff. Obviously, such a procedure controls entrance to the campus and is a serious attempt to minimize the chances for removal of children from the building by unauthorized persons. One principal has a lock-down procedure that involves a single designated entryway for parents to gain access to the school and a preassigned place for them to wait while the children are being summoned for release. The emergency fact card on each child is then pulled and consulted before any student is released to an adult. This principal noted that although this is a long and cumbersome process, it insures the safety of the children.

Insuring optimal effectiveness of response in an emergency is the premise underlying crisis team management. Team members, therefore, should be assigned roles and responsibilities commensurate with their training and experience. If training for a variety of possibilities has been properly conducted during the initial stages of team formation, team members will be equipped with sufficient skills to handle their responsibilities. Effective team training should be focused on developing a procedure for calling the team together, gathering information about the crisis, formulating a systematic plan for response, and assigning roles and responsibilities.

Mobilizing resources. Once the team has assessed the crisis and made a preliminary determination of the needed level of response, procedures can be implemented for calling upon resources to aid crisis resolution. If team members have produced a comprehensive crisis response manual, then this document would include a list of available resources. Some resources are the usual types of public emergency response agencies, such as fire and police departments, while other resources are semi- or nonpublic hospitals and mental health professionals. Depending upon the nature of these agencies and the types of professionals, there may be a need to maintain periodic contact to insure a smooth and effective response. It may be helpful to call or visit these resources on a yearly or semiannual basis. This contact might involve asking the agency or person to participate in some aspect of team training, for example, asking a psychologist to work with the team on one of the simulation exercises in Appendix C.

When calling upon resources to aid in crisis response, the team needs to have a very clear idea of the scope and level of authority of everyone involved. For example, if the police or fire department personnel are called in on an emergency, they automatically assume full authority until the immediate crisis is resolved. There may be other instances, however, where the team retains authority and directs the overall crisis response. Whatever the situation, team members must be clear about (1) who is in control, (2) the point at which control is given over to another authority, and (3) the point where their control is reassumed.

There will probably be several points in a major crisis where team authority will change, depending upon the resources involved. For example, if the emergency is a major fire involving a large portion of the school building, the team will surrender authority to fire and police officials for a long period of time, but will probably retain authority over the students and their release to parents. Later the team will reassume authority and responsibility for either returning the building to a usable form or identifying an alternate space for classroom use. Then there may be a need to use additional outside resources to work with students and staff who are traumatized from witnessing people injured by or killed in the fire. Once again, the team's authority may be somewhat diminished as other professionals assume responsibility for handling this aspect of the crisis response. Even in this situation, however, the crisis team will monitor those who are responding to student and staff needs and will step in quickly if it becomes apparent that a resource is not acting appropriately.

Summary

Crisis response calls for a coordinated, well-planned effort by all team members. The team needs to clearly understand the delineation of roles and responsibilities during crisis response and to follow a preestablished plan of returning the school as nearly as possible to its precrisis state. This chapter gave details of a process to achieve that goal.

Chapter 5

The Catholic School Principal Manages Crisis

The differences between the roles of Catholic and public school principals quickly emerge in the context of managing a crisis. A public school principal usually follows procedures dictated by a central administrative bureaucracy that constrains the administrator's actions but does offer resources to aid in crisis resolution. By contrast, a Catholic school principal frequently has little direction and support from outside the immediate environment of the school, a factor due largely to the organizational structure of Catholic schools.

This chapter focuses on assessing the degree of direction and support a principal may have in handling a crisis, and on how to respond accordingly. The assumption of the later sections of this chapter is that minimal direction and support are offered by a central schools office. This is not intended as criticism; rather, it sets the scene as it is and then points the direction for developing resources for crisis response.

Assessing for Response

To make the most appropriate response to an emergency, it is necessary to assess and ascertain the levels of support that can be expected from various administrative bodies. As suggested previously, the principal needs to consult the diocesan administrative handbook to determine if procedures and policies are provided for crisis response. Once this is done, a follow-up measure should be a call to the superintendent's office to find out whether any additional resources are available.

Obviously, when a procedure is clearly outlined in the diocesan administrative handbook, the school's plans for crisis response need to be tailored to conform with that procedure. For example, the diocese may have a public-information officer who deals with the media on all matters affecting diocesan affairs. This means that the parish elementary school must make plans to call upon that officer in an emergency to act as spokesperson. The diocese may already have a procedure for notifying central office personnel in an emergency. Accordingly, the local school's crisis response plan should include this as part of its overall planning.

If the diocesan schools office has area coordinators or supervisors, the principal should discuss with them details of plans for formulating a crisis response manual. Particular focus should be on what is often termed "need to know," which means the local administrator will want to know the level of crisis that requires informing the coordinator or supervisor. The normal response is that if the site administrator can resolve the issue, do so. It is good public relations and a good rule of thumb for the principal to involve the central office in any issue that has the potential for or does involve legal action.

If no clear diocesan policy exists for handling emergencies, the principal is basically left to develop a procedure for the school. Concerning a notification procedure, it is important to notify diocesan officials, and the pastor if it is a parish elementary school, very early in a crisis. This procedure needs to be clearly stated in the emergency handbook.

As any principal who has faced such a situation knows, nothing so undermines the morale of those involved in a crisis and the ultimate confidence parents and students place in school administrators as when someone other than the principal takes control. The unwanted message is that matters are being mishandled and a more competent authority needs to take charge. Working in advance to clarify responsibilities and lines of authority may help to avoid this outcome.

The Principal's Role During Emergencies

While other school personnel may have preassigned functions to handle in an emergency, the school's principal, as the chief administrative officer, has responsibility for directing crisis response. This responsibility should be delegated to someone else only in those instances where the principal is incapacitated by the emergency or is away from the school when a crisis occurs. These possibilities can be covered in planning. For example, if the principal, while accompanying students on a field trip, is injured in a serious accident, then someone else from the school would have to take charge of directing crisis response. One suggested order of authority is principal, vice principal, and head secretary.

Directing crisis response means, primarily, coordinating a team activity. The major stumbling block for the principal to avoid is getting caught up in doing many of the things that can be handled by other team members. Writing out and placing name tags on children during an emergency, for example, is a task best delegated to someone else. Depending upon the seriousness of the emergency and the degree of total school involvement, the principal needs to function in a triage model, making decisions regarding which needs should receive most critical attention and which ones can be left until later.

Coordinating response. The principal's role in an emergency should mirror the administrator's day-to-day role as school leader. An effective principal works at providing optimal conditions for others to do their jobs—for teachers to teach. During an emergency, it is essential for the principal, as crisis team leader, to focus on coordinating functions to allow others to handle a large portion of the many aspects of crisis response that will arise. If the principal gets caught up in handling a plethora of minor matters, the result would be loss of control of the situation. A good illustration is that of a fire department battalion chief. The battalion chief does not pick up the water hose and go charging into a burning building; rather, this firefighter's role is to capture the overall picture of the fire suppression effort, thus focusing on directing the efforts of others. Obviously, there are times when a battalion chief would pick up a hose and fight the fire, but those instances are reserved for the direst of circumstances, when a firefighter's life is in serious jeopardy and the chief is the last available person capable of responding.

The principal's role in a crisis is best described as coordinator of the response effort. The principal must be able to move quickly and decisively to assess the emergency, to work with other team members in assigning their tasks, and to plan an appropriate response.

Establishing channels of communication. Having accurate information on the nature of an emergency is of paramount importance in dealing with a crisis. The principal, therefore, needs to concentrate efforts on creating channels of communication that provide access to timely, accurate information.

A striking example of information that did not get through is the oft-cited example of the Kennedy administration's handling of the Bay of Pigs crisis. Evidently, several key members of the crisis management team planning for the Cuban invasion did not believe the effort would be successful. These key members were military personnel whose years of experience provided a font of important information, yet they held back voicing their reservations lest they be judged as being negative, as not being "team players." Their reluctance to speak up and provide vital information resulted in disaster.

The point is that the principal needs to have not only accurate information but also, when invited, the opinions of individuals whose experience can add substantively to decisions on how best to proceed in handling an emergency.

The principal also must be able to give accurate information on what has occurred and how plans are being formulated for crisis response. The administrator will need to provide information to parents, in particular, and to other school personnel, church officials, diocesan school personnel, and, possibly, the media. At times, questions will be raised concerning issues or problems about which school officials have inadequate or a complete lack of information. The best response is to say that one doesn't know. Avoid giving the "no comment" response because it may be interpreted as an attempt to be deceptive and cause the media to lose trust in the spokesperson. Neither the principal's interests nor those of the school community are served by such a response. Telling the questioner that information regarding a particular matter is being gathered and will be made available as soon as possible is the most appropriate response.

We all make mistakes, and this is especially true when working in the pressure-cooker atmosphere of crisis management. People working under great duress make errors even though they have the best intentions, and these mistakes need to be acknowledged once they become known. Rather than being a sign of weakness or unprofessionalism, acknowledging a mistake can do much to diffuse a potentially volatile situation.

Working with parents. Any child-care worker knows that nothing brings out the wrath and irrational behavior of parents like an emergency involving a perceived threat to their children. This is just a natural, protective instinct. Thus, parents who come to the school during a crisis need to be dealt with calmly yet firmly. School officials must convey a clear message that matters are under control and everyone is acting in the children's best interests.

During a crisis, access to areas of the grounds and buildings should be restricted for everyone's safety and well-being. If possible, parents should be moved to an area or room that is away from the media, a place where they will not be subjected to media scrutiny while breaking down or expressing misgivings about the competence of the school's administration to handle the crisis.

At some point it may be necessary to meet with parents as a group to explain what has occurred and how it is being handled. This type of meeting can be very emotional and draining for all involved. Again, it is important to hold such meetings in an area shielded from the press and other media. Parents should have the opportunity to ask questions and raise concerns in a secure atmosphere, free of cameras and reporters.

In meeting with parents, questions and suggestions may arise about restricting access to the campus (e.g., locking doors, posting security guards) to prevent a future occurrence. While all of these questions may be legitimate, there is also a balanced concern for the general welfare of the school community. Schools cannot be locked down like prisons; there has to be reasonable freedom of movement for all. Although a visitor policy may be in effect, in a free society if someone is going to commit a random act of violence, the terrible truth is that they are probably going to succeed. Schools, like other public institutions, unfortunately are vulnerable targets for random acts of violence.

Handling media relations. Print- and electronic-media representatives are quick to respond to emergencies, since nothing feeds the appetite of the local evening newscast like footage of children involved in a tragedy. Critiques of local television news have documented the amount of coverage given to stories involving violence. The question facing school officials in a crisis is not whether they can escape media scrutiny, since they seldom can, but how they can best deal with the media when coping with an emergency.

The first step, which needs to be carried out long before a crisis occurs, is to find out whether the diocese has a public-information officer. This individual is specially trained and experienced in dealing with the media and can be a valuable asset in an emergency. The public-information officer should be contacted in the early phase of crisis-team formation with a request for information on how that office can assist the team in an emergency. The response may be that a policy precludes involvement in a parish school crisis, although such a reply would be a bit far-fetched. Most likely, the public-information officer will welcome an opportunity to share information and suggestions with the team. To reiterate a point made earlier, this person may be most willing to cooperate if there are several teams training simultaneously, thus providing a forum to address a large group.

If there is no public-information officer available through the diocese or if the officer is unwilling to get involved on the local parish-school level, the crisis team will need to plan accordingly. In such cases, all dealings with the news media should come through the team or its designated representative, and this choice should be made in advance. The media have a need for news, and if information is not coming from school officials, then anyone available will be interviewed—even children or other school personnel—to get information about the crisis. Moving quickly to establish a spokesperson will give school administrators much greater control over the reporting and interpreting of events in the local news. The principal is the logical person to fill this role.

School officials have a right to restrict media access to the school and grounds, and plans can be made to restrict media representatives to an area of the building or an area adjacent to the school. Thinking more positively, the team may explore ways to provide an area for media personnel that includes space to work and some refreshments. Whatever area is chosen for the media, make sure that it is away from the room where the team meets. Media reps should not be privy to the conversations taking place among team members or be allowed to photograph the room where team meetings are held, an area that might contain sensitive material posted on wall charts or notes scribbled on papers lying on tables.

The principal needs to have sufficient and accurate information about the crisis before meeting with media reps. It is important to convey to the media a message that the situation is under control, and one way of doing this is by portraying accurately what has occurred. The more facts administrators are able to provide in as timely a manner as possible, the more they will remain in control of what appears on the nightly newscast or in the local newspaper. If it is too early to know exactly what precipitated the emergency, then only a very brief statement should be made to the media, indicating that information is being gathered and that someone will be back to talk with them as soon as the information is available. The principal should then terminate the news conference without answering any questions.

It is important to be quite careful about releasing names of children who are involved in the crisis. School officials need to be aware of laws regarding privacy of information in school records. Moreover, nothing could be worse than having parents find out via the television newscast that sons and daughters are injured or even dead as the result of a school emergency. Such information obviously should be conveyed in private and away from news coverage.

Even in the middle of a crisis, school officials should remember that the media represent the best vehicle for communicating a positive message about the school to parents and the general community. That message basically should (1) acknowledge an emergency has taken place, (2) confirm that everyone at the school is working to insure the safety and well-being of students, and (3) assure that the school will return to normal as soon as possible.

Getting back to normal. Everything the principal and team members do in dealing with an emergency is directed at getting the school back to normal. This involves resolving the crisis in the best manner possible; attending to the needs of children, staff, and any affected parents; and returning to the normal schedule of daily events. Buildings restored as much as possible to their precrisis condition, with teachers and students in classrooms carrying on the daily routine, will do much to alleviate the sense of an unresolved emergency.

At times, children whose lives have been disrupted by a crisis will act out or exhibit aberrant behaviors. It is imperative that administrators and teachers pay careful attention to this behavior. This needs to be done, however, in as unobtrusive a manner as possible and in a manner demonstrating sensitivity to the children's needs. The message that needs to be clear, consistent, and carried through is that the situation is returning to normal and that everyone is going to be okay.

An evenhanded yet firmly administered discipline policy works best to convince children that the school is returning to normal. School officials may think that when people, particularly children, have been under enormous stress, the best procedure might be to relax school policy while the school is readjusting and returning to normal day-to-day functioning. Although it may be common sense to follow this procedure for a day or two, the full-discipline policy should be implemented as quickly as possible. Children need to know that they are cared for by adults who show their love and concern by working to contain the children's disruptive behavior. Children whose behavior is allowed to go unchecked are given a direct message that the adults are not caring for them.

Experience indicates that it takes some people longer than others to resolve a crisis and return to a sense of normalcy. This is especially true with children, who may suffer lingering effects of trauma resulting from an emergency. The task is to seek a balance between moving ahead and the need to stop to attend to unresolved issues resulting from the crisis.

In planning a return to the regular school schedule, it may be necessary to take a day off from school between the time the crisis is resolved and classes are resumed. This break may help give everyone something of a psychological breather and help prepare them for the return to a normal schedule. The most important thing is to direct all efforts toward a return to things as they were before the crisis. The more quickly this is accomplished, the sooner the process of healing can take place.

In returning to the regular schedule, it also may be necessary, depending upon the nature of the crisis, to allow parents to walk through the school building to reassure themselves that all is well. This would be best carried out before the resumption of classes, not while classes are in progress. After all, the staff would not want parents walking into classrooms during the day, since this would be not only disruptive but also out of the regular routine.

Caring for the caregivers. While they are focusing on the needs of students, teachers, parents, and staff, the principal and other team members may fail to recognize the effects of the crisis on themselves. At some point, the team may need to set aside time for their own healing to take place. Those who have worked so diligently to resolve the crisis may discover a need, frequently ignored, for some intervention of their own. The team, therefore, may want to consider ways to resolve their own issues resulting from the crisis event. Such means may range from some form of group counseling or a very private complaint session to a party that allows everyone to blow off steam.

Concern for the caregivers goes beyond team members to include teachers and other school staff. It is important to monitor everyone within the school for difficulty in coping with stress. As pointed out earlier, this vulnerability may not become evident until the crisis has been resolved. One of the best means for dealing with this situation is to hold a closed-door meeting, open to any staff member and facilitated by an outside consultant. The purpose is to allow everyone who has been in a caregiver role an opportunity to express whatever they may wish to say about the events that have taken place. Anyone who has participated in or helped run such a session can speak to the power of healing that takes place within these meetings.

Such meetings offer a perfect opportunity to incorporate prayer and scripture into the process, allowing the healing power of faith to come to full expression. The movement of the Spirit within a group gathered in prayer should be emphasized at this time. This group can provide that environment where the Spirit moans in healing the hurt and pain that has been sustained during the crisis.

Summary

This chapter focused on the vital role played by the principal in a crisis, with the premise that no one else is better equipped to take on the role of crisis manager. Suggestions were offered for handling specific issues that can arise in an emergency, and the chapter concluded with a brief discussion of the need to take care of those charged with responsibility in a crisis.

Chapter 6

The Catholic School Teacher Manages Crisis

A well-trained classroom teacher is one of the most knowledgeable persons when it comes to dealing with children during a crisis. A significant part of the teacher's day is spent handling a number of minor crises and, on occasion, a major one. Most crises can be handled by teachers who possess the skills and confidence to manage an emergency, and the effectiveness of a teacher trained in crisis response is firmly established (Taylor, Brady, & Swank, 1991).

Training for Teachers

This chapter discusses training to help the teaching staff prevent and handle crises and their effects. The discussion includes crises arising within the classroom and those that originate outside the confines of the classroom setting, involving more than an individual student or even a group of students.

Crises in the classroom. For emergencies arising within the classroom, the most important consideration is having a means for the teacher to call for assistance. This may be some form of signaling device that allows the teacher to easily notify the office that an emergency exists. An alternate method might be to have a student go to the office or to the next classroom to summon help, but this can involve wasted time and, depending upon the student's age, a lot of miscommunication.

Whatever type of communication signaling device is chosen for notifying school officials that an emergency exists, it needs to be practiced in drill form so teachers become familiar with it. A yearly review of emergency procedures for teachers might include an opportunity for a teacher to practice this drill with colleagues, who could offer suggestions and comments for improving crisis management techniques.

An earlier chapter focused on the need for the crisis management team to survey the school property to prevent possible crises; the same need exists for the classroom teacher. Teachers should participate in periodic inservice training to update their knowledge of the types of accidents and emergencies that can occur within the classroom and of the appropriate preventive measures they can take. A discussion led by an experienced classroom teacher is one of the easiest ways to achieve this goal. The sharing of experiences among teachers speaks louder than any other form of training, for no one understands the world of a classroom teacher better than a colleague.

This leads to an important point. Whatever procedures are developed for handling crises, it is critical that teachers review them and offer input before they are finalized. Teachers become the key personnel in a crisis, and having their input in developing crisis procedures can prove invaluable from a practical and a public-relations point of view. A major complaint heard from teachers is that frequently school policies are developed that have a major impact on them with little consideration given to their views. Teachers often complain of silly rules and regulations that seem far removed from the reality of their everyday experience. Procedures for handling crises are far too important not to have understanding and support from teachers. Asking for feedback before finalizing a procedure can help improve morale and save the administrator embarrassment when faced with questions concerning faults found with a policy that has been promulgated.

Crises outside the classroom. The second type of crisis arises outside the classroom and involves the entire school. Such a crisis would necessitate individual classroom teachers working with other school personnel to move children away from danger and to preassigned areas. Fires, earthquakes, and tornados are but three of many types of crises that call for specific procedures to protect the children. Teachers, therefore, need to be familiar with the appropriate emergency procedures.

Of course, there are other types of crises that might arise that do not necessitate moving children from the building yet require the sustained efforts of teachers well prepared to deal with them in the most effective way possible.

Determining the nature of a crisis. The staff must be able to determine which matters can best be handled by a single teacher and which require outside resources. A teacher who is feeling overwhelmed and is on the verge of panic in attempting to deal with a classroom emergency needs to call for backup assistance. On the other hand, if a teacher feels confident in dealing with a situation, then later notification to school officials for the purpose of proper communication would suffice. Training that focuses on helping teachers assess the level of danger in a crisis and on giving them procedures for summoning assistance and reporting emergencies is time well spent. Procedures for exiting classrooms and buildings should be so well practiced as to be routine.

Addressing the long-term effects of crisis. In addition to being able to respond to an immediate emergency, teachers need strategies to help students cope with the long-term effects of a past crisis. Helping students deal with feelings of fear and loss is an important part of crisis training for teachers.

To help children work through moments of crisis, teachers should be encouraged to call upon that wonderful fund of experience they have as instructional leaders. Teachers have spent years focusing on how best to help children learn, a question that can be modified in helping children deal with the long-term effects of trauma.

Knowledge alone does not make for an outstanding classroom instructor; rather, it is the creative, innovative teacher who can assume the learner's perspective and understand the difficulties of attempting to master new concepts or material who is judged to be highly effective in the classroom. Thus, the same mastery of technique can be employed to help children deal with crisis events. The teacher who can understand the child's perspective on the issue—how the child sees the world and how the child thinks—is a person who can assist youngsters in working through trauma.

Just as teachers call upon various techniques in instruction, be it cooperative learning or problem-solving strategies, to name but two, so too can they use these methods with children who have experienced a crisis. For example, a small-group discussion could deal with feelings children are having about a seriously ill classmate who is receiving chemotherapy. The experience of sharing their anxieties, along with the chance to engage in problem-solving around the questions of what to say to or how to play with their classmate, can be extremely helpful to children as they voice their fears and hear that others have the same feelings.

Chapter 8 presents a detailed discussion on using counseling professionals in crises. It may be helpful here, however, to discuss briefly how a counselor can work with the classroom teacher. Although counselors are trained primarily to work with individual students and groups of students, these professionals can also help the teacher devise strategies for the classroom. This collaboration is best illustrated by the teacher and counselor who work together to devise a writing or creative art project on feelings the children have following the death of a classmate's parent. The teacher and counselor will need to discuss the children's cognitive development level, the ways in which children express feelings, and how to explore the meaning of whatever product is produced. Working with children in this way can be a richly rewarding experience, as the teacher watches the students express and begin to work through feelings of fear, guilt, and anger. With the counselor as a resource, the teacher can then focus on students' needs.

Finding support during and following a crisis. A teacher's first concern is always for the student. This nurturing spirit is encouraged during training, although some might maintain it is an instinctual, deep-seated part of the personality of all good teachers. Whatever its origin, student welfare is the teacher's primary focus.

In a crisis, the teacher's needs can become so deeply repressed that it may be very difficult even to acknowledge they exist. Only much later does the recognition dawn of what experts have identified as the long-term effects of stress: chronic lack of energy, a general loss of enthusiasm for teaching, angry outbursts out of proportion to events, and vague physical symptoms and illnesses. These symptoms become the only means the body has for communicating the degree of psychological and physical deterioration resulting from the long-repressed effects of the crisis. When this explanation is presented to teachers, it frequently strikes a chord of understanding, as they begin to recognize a link between the crisis and their symptoms.

Teachers, or anyone else for that matter, cannot be part of an event where children are killed, maimed, injured, and/or psychologically traumatized and not also be traumatized to some degree. I remember a discussion that took place nearly twenty years ago with a physician who had been part of a medical team sent to a plane crash site. There was nothing the medical personnel could do to relieve suffering, since everyone on the plane had been killed. Emergency personnel responding to the crash site, therefore, were called upon to collect dead bodies. The physician reflected on the months following the crash, when everyone on the medical team experienced nightmares filled with images of dismembered bodies. If trained medical personnel can be traumatized by suffering and death, is it any wonder that teachers and other child-care workers would have similar experiences following a school emergency?

The point here is clear: While it is necessary and appropriate to tend to children's needs in a crisis, teachers must be aware of their own needs, lest these helpers end up so immobilized they are ineffective in an emergency. How can this possibility be avoided? First, teachers should be aware of and acknowledge the possible effects of stress. Second, teachers must realize that effective steps can be taken to deal with stress, even something as simple as having a trusted colleague keep a watchful eye to warn of apparent deterioration from stress.

Learning to call for assistance of any kind can also be helpful as a stress-reducing measure. For example, requesting additional teaching assistants or extended time for a teaching assistant in the classroom each day can help reduce stress. Taking time away from the school and going to a place where one can feel free to laugh, cry, or express whatever feelings are present is also important. Norman Cousins has so eloquently pointed out how frequently people overlook the psychological and physical healing effects of laughter. The point is to recognize what works for the individual in reducing stress and then to feel free to utilize this means so that the teacher may be an effective helper to the students.

Summary

Teachers are the frontline troops in a crisis involving children in a school setting. This chapter focused on measures teachers can implement to head off the possibility of crisis in the classroom and pointed out the need for training to equip them with skills needed to handle an emergency. Later, the focus was on how teachers can respond to the ongoing needs of children who have experienced trauma and on precautions teachers need to remember so they can avoid becoming so caught up in the crisis that they are immobilized and ineffective as helpers. Suggestions were offered regarding stress management needs.

Chapter 7

Crisis Response: A Call to Faith

Any school, public or Catholic, faced with an emergency has a responsibility to respond in the most appropriate manner to the needs of children, staff, and parents. Whether it is a public suburban school, equipped with the very latest in educational technology, or an inner-city Catholic school, dependent on the generosity of local merchants for donations of paper for the duplicator, when responding to children in need of emergency medical services, these schools would probably be indistinguishable. It is only in the later stages of crisis response that schools begin to sharply define their differences. While public schools seek the overall well-being of students and utilize appropriate tools to carry out this mission, Catholic schools, by their very nature, seek also to address the religious dimension of students' lives, a dimension the public school is not permitted to acknowledge. This chapter discusses how Catholic schools go about filling this need and adding to the overall crisis response.

Although they lack the financial and other resources of public schools, Catholic schools have a religious dimension as a tool to incorporate into the overall planning and response a crisis team makes. This tool is as valuable as any other resource utilized in emergency response.

Faith Response to Crisis

Chapter 2 discussed the development and contents of the crisis response manual, tailored to the needs of the school. One of the more important sections in this manual is a statement concerning the faith dimension of the school. This statement should have two thrusts. The first is a reflection on statements drawn from other school documents concerning the school's mission of faith development. The second evolves from the first, addressing how crisis response fits into the school's overall mission of faith development. This statement does not need to be elaborate or involved, only a parsimonious reflection that serves as a foundation for the school's action during crisis response.

How the school utilizes faith in response to a crisis depends largely upon the nature of the event and the ages of the children involved. Two examples might help to illustrate this point: a seventh grader who suffers an injury on the playground that requires a brief hospital stay and a third grader who dies as the result of an automobile accident. While these incidents differ markedly in severity, they also differ in regard to the way in which school officials will address them with the students. Seventh graders are at a much different level of cognitive development than third graders and will therefore require a response tailored to their needs.

How the team should proceed in formulating a response to children's needs in the faith dimension can best be answered by reviewing the various religion texts used by the school. A well-thought-out religious education program uses texts focusing children on issues that make sense to them. Then, through a series of exercises and projects, the children are able to place this new learning within a larger scheme. For example, a discussion on God's friendship with us begins with the friendships we have in our daily lives and then goes on to point us toward demonstrating God's friendship for others through our service of, say, the homeless.

Negative Messages

While faith is important when dealing with questions of crisis, it is equally important to dispel myths that can easily lead children to experience unnecessary guilt. For example, children are quick to pick up on the notion that if something evil or bad has occurred, then someone must have done something wrong and is being punished for it. In this instance, God can be seen as punishing a particular child, a class, or even the whole school. Crisis then is identified with the wrath of God. It is very important to deal with this issue head-on and to raise it very early in the crisis. Children need to hear that the event did not occur because God was angry with someone.

The two dangers addressed here are that a child may think God acts in a wrathful manner and that a child may assume personal responsibility for what has occurred ("God is mad because the other day I took something that did not belong to me and now I'm being punished"). Children often conclude that their parents are divorcing because they, the children, have done something wrong. Strange as it may seem, this reasoning is employed frequently by children to explain why bad things happen. Although religious belief can negatively influence a person's interpretation of an experience, it also can be a positive force as someone grapples with a crisis. Religious belief can be a powerful tool, when used appropriately, to help children who are faced with a crisis that threatens to overwhelm them.

Keeping the Focus

The faith dimension aspect of the school's mission statement can be especially useful in helping children to focus on two central themes: first, we are all part of something that is larger than just ourselves; second, our God is a loving God. These themes are simple and straightforward, as they are intended to be. It is important, especially in a crisis, to keep the message simple and direct because this works best to help children achieve healing in their lives. Complicated theological explanations for life and death are not appropriate at this time. Remember what people are seeking, be they children, adolescents or adults: some consolation to nurture and support them in this moment of crisis.

Just as the crisis team works diligently on other aspects of crisis resolution, so should it work on how to appeal to children's faith within the context of a disruptive event. An understanding of cognitive development theory can be extremely helpful to adults faced with the challenge of assisting children to deal with overwhelming issues (Ault, 1983; Bjorklund, 1989).

Teachable Moments

Young children often have what may appear to adults to be bizarre ways of stating theological realities. It is important to remember that while adults are capable of thinking in abstract and theoretical ways, children have to deal with the world in a concrete manner. At times, children will focus on a peculiar aspect of a problem, as when a group of second graders wondered if a dead classmate might need his textbooks. After all, he may be in heaven, but he still must be going to school, right?

If we stop for a moment and think about what the children in this case were asking, we can see tremendous possibilities for a "teachable moment," those opportunities good teachers wait to seize. Teachers relish those opportunities when a youngster or teenager has asked what at first seemed to be a question coming out of left field, or one based on something that happened that morning on the way to school or on some current news event. Whatever the question's genesis, creative teachers have learned to put aside the prepared lesson plan and use this opportunity to do some real teaching. The gifted teacher knows to look for those times when learners are most open to the possibility of understanding and then motivates students to make that leap forward. Just as Jesus did! He seized a particular moment and brought grace to those who were listening, whether it was the time when the apostles were arguing amongst themselves over who was the more important, or when there were so many hungry mouths to feed and so little bread to feed them, or during the dawning twilight following a long night of fishing when the apostles had little to show for their efforts other than empty nets. All of these became teachable moments, times when the Lord demonstrated the power of grace to effect change.

Good therapists learn to utilize a process called reframing as they work with clients. Sometimes a client is stuck in negative thinking or sees life as totally hopeless, and the therapist will challenge the client to look at the problem in a different way. When this technique has worked, the surprised look on the client's face is all the reward the therapist needs, for it can do so much to move a person who is "stuck" in therapy.

The same technique can work for administrators and teachers. When they are stuck in the midst of all the grief and agony that can accompany a crisis, they need to learn to reframe the issues, and a beginning point in that process is when someone asks, "How can this situation be turned into a teachable, grace-filled moment?" Keeping an eye out for teachable moments and a time when the Lord can be asked to bring grace to what appears to be a terrible tragedy can help to start the healing process. All that is required is to keep alert.

Summary

Following a crisis, faith can be a powerful ally in the healing process. This chapter examined various ways the school can use faith to address a crisis event, with emphasis placed on recognizing children's levels of cognitive development. Cautions were presented against allowing negative aspects of belief to creep into the response to emergencies. Finally, reframing the issue of crisis was suggested as a way to turn it into a teachable moment.

Chapter 8

Psychological Support Systems

Many of the emergencies that arise in schools will eventually require some type of psychological intervention for everyone, including students, staff, parents, and administrators. Frequently the need for such intervention is overlooked or discounted, especially when the focus is on helping adults who are busy attending to children's needs and ignoring their own fears, failures, and deep sense of loss. This chapter offers a systematic plan for developing this type of support system, so that it may be implemented in a crisis and serve as a preventive step in anticipating crises.

Preventive Programming

The availability of counseling services for students will vary greatly among Catholic schools. Most high schools provide a systematic counseling program to students; however, elementary schools generally do not make such programs available. Possibly, this is due mostly to tighter funding restrictions at the elementary school level. There may also be a failure to recognize the need for such services at the elementary level, coupled with a historic absence of counseling in elementary schools. Whatever the reason, one has only to visit an elementary school counselor's office to see the critical role this professional staff member plays.

The counselor's role is vital when it involves providing consultation services to teachers and prevention programs for students. I recall, for example, a visit to the counseling office of a local public elementary school to observe the weekly session of a group of fourth grade boys. The boys, focused on the impact of parental divorce and the difficulty of living in a single-parent household, were welcoming a new member to the group. They shared their own concerns and acted as appropriate models to this youngster, who was experiencing a lot of stress and feelings of isolation as he attempted to cope with his parents' recent marital breakup.

Although many Catholic elementary schools are not able to have a full-time counselor on staff, they are able to bring in someone on a part-time basis or to implement group programs using paraprofessionals and volunteers. While nothing substitutes for a credentialed counselor who has been trained to respond to the many issues children in crisis face, some type of organized program can help to meet the needs of children as they try to cope with their issues.

The first concern, then, is preventive programming to head off crises. Even in a school with minimal resources, a crisis assessment should include examining the need for preventive programs. The team should begin not by focusing on the lack of resources, but by asking what needs exist within the school. Once the needs have been identified, consider how they can be addressed. Schools frequently find that the process of pinpointing needs allows innovative and creative solutions to surface. For example, one Catholic elementary school secured the services of a counselor from a neighboring Catholic high school, who met weekly with a group of boys experiencing behavioral problems in classes. The high school provided the counselor at no cost to the elementary school. What is important here is that the need was met because the grade school principal first recognized there was a need, identified an appropriate resource for help, and then requested assistance.

Recently, when a principal had to identify resources to help students and staff deal with a crisis that had affected the entire school, she called upon a local hospital for help, which included the services of staff psychologists specially trained in crisis management. This administrator began her search by identifying the types of agencies and institutions best able to respond to crises—what better place than the local hospital?

An elementary school principal, who also is a credentialed counselor, addressed the need for counseling services in her school by utilizing the services of several interns from a nearby university. With few financial resources to spend, she soon had a fully functioning intervention program consisting of individual counseling for the most troubled students, group counseling for students experiencing classroom behavior problems, and a parenting skills program. This is an outstanding example of a creative approach to addressing needs, instead of looking at the problem and concluding that a lack of financial resources precludes any viable solution.

Identifying needs and seeking resources for or creative responses to those needs are appropriate tasks for the crisis management team. This type of problem-solving can be a fertile training ground for the team as it works through its initial period of training and preparation for response to emergencies. As the team works in this area, with no pressure to make decisions quickly, there is an opportunity to learn about the differing styles of each member. Any learning that occurs in this less-charged atmosphere can only work to the team's advantage as it progresses toward that time when it may be working under great duress.

Utilizing Outside Resources

It is important to recognize the limitations school personnel have while training to respond to specific issues arising during a crisis, and this is especially true in the area of psychological support services for those who have been directly or indirectly involved in an emergency. The team will need to address this area carefully and seek the most competent assistance available.

Basically there are three general sources of professionals who can help in addressing psychological support for victims of trauma: a neighboring college or university with interns in its counselor training program, private-practice professionals, and public and local governmental agencies.

Most colleges and universities have either departments or schools of education that include counselor training programs. These programs frequently have professors specially trained in crisis intervention who would welcome the opportunity to consult with the crisis management team as it begins setting up an intervention program. These programs also have students in the latter stages of program work who are preparing for field experience. Such a counselor training program is an excellent resource to call upon either when an emergency response requires bringing in counselors to work with students and staff or when the team wants to implement a series of preventive-type intervention strategies. It is important to remember that any intern working with students and staff must receive proper supervision; therefore, the team will need to carefully discuss this matter with the institution's intern supervisor.

Many Catholic schools rely on a group of private-practice mental health providers as referral resources for students experiencing difficulties at school or at home. These mental health professionals usually are willing to meet with the staff and to discuss their concerns, especially such matters as forming a crisis intervention team. Having an outside professional to assist the team provides an opportunity to observe firsthand this professional's work, which will be helpful when deciding who would work best with groups of students, parents, and staff during an actual crisis.

The third potential resource is public or governmental agencies. The team may find that a state-funded mental health clinic, for example, has outreach services that provide limited training for the team and/or direct services to children traumatized by a crisis. A prearranged visit to the clinic, instead of a letter or phone call, is suggested as the basis for establishing a professional relationship with the clinic staff that will leave them more open to responding to the school in an emergency. Counseling is also provided by local emergency medical services (EMS) units, which are often a regular part of a fire department's response. These units have highly trained professionals who are focused on crisis response and can offer valuable tips for handling an emergency. Their aid can be particularly helpful with large groups of children who may need some form of immediate, short-term assistance to deal with trauma following a catastrophic event.

Another source of support within this third category is the local hospital, as has been illustrated earlier. Although the medical center may be privately operated, often its staff include mental health professionals who consider it part of their public-service responsibility to respond to schools and similar institutions. A call or visit to the hospital may prove valuable in gaining assistance with crisis response team training or in identifying resources for a crisis.

The goal of planning in this area is a well-conceptualized idea of how the team will call upon psychological support resources during an emergency. This means having names and telephone numbers readily accessible—in the emergency response guide—and having some sense of how each resource will help the team address specific aspects of a crisis.

Dealing with a Crisis

Having explored available psychological support resources and identified those most appropriate for the school's needs, the team is now in a position to employ them for maximum benefit during a crisis.

The goal is to target areas where psychological support may be appropriate. For example, it may be best to have someone work alongside the team during an actual crisis or at various points in a crisis. This could be especially helpful as the team is formulating a response for dealing with an emergency. Having someone from outside the situation present to offer ideas and suggestions can give the team fresh insights into dealing with a crisis. At the same time, the team needs to be careful not to abrogate its responsibility and turn over crisis management to this outside resource. To do so would be to hopelessly complicate what is already a chaotic situation. At all times, the team must be clear about lines of responsibility. While some tasks may be delegated to others, the team, working under the principal's leadership, must maintain control of the crisis response.

A particular crisis may warrant bringing in counselors or psychologists to meet with groups of students. Although this measure has become a ubiquitous response to crises, such intervention has been shown to be particularly effective in dealing with traumatic situations such as suicide (Kalafat, 1990; Kneisel & Richards, 1988; Siehl, 1990).

During a crisis it may be beneficial to have a trained psychotherapist hold a session for parents to help them process feelings and adopt strategies for dealing with their children. The team may decide not to be directly involved in these meetings and choose instead to take on an observer role to gauge parent reaction that, in turn, may be helpful in crafting future interventions.

When implementing strategies to help those affected by a crisis, it is important to address staff needs. As pointed out earlier, the staff can easily be overlooked or forgotten during a crisis, resulting in an increase of stress-related problems among them after the emergency is resolved. Anticipating the needs of this group through small-group meetings led by counseling professionals is often the best way to head off problems that might occur as a delayed reaction to stress.

Summary

This chapter discussed using outside psychological resources during a crisis. The focus was on describing the types of counseling resources available, identifying agencies that might supply help, and determining how best to use these resources. Attention was drawn to the need to provide psychological support for all members of the school community, including teachers and other staff within the school.

Chapter 9

Parents in Time of Crisis

The backbone of a school's existence, particularly that of a Catholic school, is parental support. Nothing speaks so positively to the community's perception of a school as parents in large numbers attending school events, helping out in lunchrooms, volunteering as playground supervisors and as teacher aids, planning and participating in fund-raising programs and school carnivals, and serving on the numerous boards and committees that keep a school functioning. On the other hand, nothing so undermines the morale and effectiveness of a school as parents who constantly nitpick the administration and teachers.

When a school is involved in a crisis, the only thing taking precedence over the need for parental support is the physical safety of the students and staff. Parents are literally the key to survival in a crisis. This chapter, therefore, focuses on techniques for managing parents during a crisis.

Experienced administrators may wish to skip over or read only portions of the following material, since a background as an administrator serves better than any book when knowledge is needed about handling meetings with parents. The material below is presented, therefore, as a guide for those readers who are looking for help in handling parent meetings following a crisis.

Parents and Their Children

The bond between most parents and their children is a visceral one. As many news accounts have documented, this bond is an instinctual urge to preserve the child's safety, even at the cost of the parent's own life. There is little wonder, then, that parents will act in ways that are apparently incongruous with their personalities when they perceive their children are in danger—no matter the danger, no matter the possibility of misperception.

That warm, outgoing parent who offers a hug at each encounter, whose handshake is genuine, and who praises the school and its staff may become in a crisis a raging, out-of-control stranger, cursing and screaming at administrators for failing to protect the children's safety.

Experienced administrators expect that occasionally parents will come into the office outraged about something that has occurred. The best the principal hopes to accomplish under the circumstances is to keep calm, get the parent into an office where the rest of the school will not be disturbed, and try to resolve the issue. Any principal who manages to handle the situation in this manner counts it as a win.

Parents and School Crisis

While one out-of-control parent is difficult to deal with, a group of parents at the school during a crisis has the potential to wreak havoc on the crisis management team's efforts to normalize school life. At each juncture in the crisis, someone on the team should be assigned to ask, "How are we dealing with parents on this?" or "What impact will this decision have on parents?" It may be helpful to assign one team member as liaison to the parents, with responsibility for answering all their questions during the crisis.

Once a crisis has occurred and parents are arriving at the school, it is important to have a place away from the front office and entryway for parents to gather. This might be an empty classroom, the gym, the auditorium, or some other large room. The goal is to get parents away from the front of the school and out of hallways. The team wants to keep parents from roaming hallways and entering classrooms where children are gathered for instruction.

Parents searching for their children and entering classrooms so they can take them home only helps to increase the overall sense of impairment and panic. While such actions are acknowledged as a result of a natural parental urge, school officials should try to convince parents that this behavior is not in the children's best interests. Plans need to be instituted, as detailed earlier, for having parents in one place and having children brought to that site for orderly release.

The presence of media is another good reason to have parents located away from the front of the school. Nothing so inflames a situation as a news broadcast showing crying, distraught parents making negative statements about the school and an incompetent administration's lack of concern for children. Such an image remains for quite a while in the memories of a news audience, and it can only harm the school. Parents may be burdened also with responsibility for having made irrational statements in a short-sighted moment of panic.

Responding to Parents' Concerns

It has been stated previously that the most effective way of dealing with parental concerns about a crisis is to provide timely, accurate information that does not violate the confidentiality or legally protected rights of others. Parents are frequently looking for a medium to release all their pent-up anxiety, fears, and frustrations over the crisis. Discussing their feelings in some type of forum can be quite healthy and help move the healing process forward for all.

In choosing to have a forum on parental concerns about the school's response to the crisis, there are several preliminary steps that will help to keep it as well controlled as possible. First, make sure that it is announced with as much advance notice as possible. The meeting should be held in the school, in a room that can accommodate the anticipated audience. To discourage satellite discussions, remove seating as the meeting time approaches and the size of the audience is gauged. If the number of participants increases, more chairs can be set up. If the meeting is taking place in a large room or auditorium, provide a specific place where parents can ask questions. Having simple refreshments for everyone to enjoy before the meeting begins is an additional housekeeping function that needs attention.

Ask the pastor and any associates to attend and to sit among the parents. Meeting with the pastor and associates beforehand to present an overview of what is planned is a good way to secure their support. Emphasize their positive support and the impact it will have on the parents.

Additional people for the meeting are other administrators, any teachers who were directly affected by the crisis or who want to attend as a sign of support (their presence is not always necessary), and other professionals who may be able to offer relevant information. This latter group may include police, fire department officials, paramedics, and psychologists or other mental health professionals. The principal should chair the meeting, unless there is some good reason not to—and there very well may be such a situation.

People to exclude are the media and the press. Unless they are convinced that there is some gain in having representatives from the media present, the team should make this a closed-door meeting. The media reps may argue to be admitted, but a private school on private property has no obligation, legal or otherwise, to admit them. Other people to exclude might be neighbors whose presence could be disruptive.

It is important to set a time limit. This is a sign of planning and of respect for the time of parents and school personnel. It is always easy to renegotiate an extension of the time limit, but it is difficult to cut off the meeting when an ending has not been set in advance. The assistant principal, one of the teachers, or even the parish priest might act as timekeeper. If things are dragging on, the timekeeper should stand up and state that the preannounced ending time has passed.

A good organizer sets an agenda for meetings. Consider writing the agenda on a chalkboard or poster board where all participants can see it. The crisis management team should rehearse, and thus be able to anticipate how the meeting will flow.

As with every meeting, a good beginning point is an introduction that includes the names and titles of everyone except the parents. Depending on group size, it may be helpful to have parents introduce themselves. A brief introductory statement can be made that includes the following: (1) details of what occurred, (2) what school officials did in responding to the crisis, and (3) what the school is doing now to get everything back to normal. For example, if the emergency involved children who were taken to the hospital as a result of some accident, the number of children and a brief statement concerning their general condition can be given. It is not helpful to go into long detail about each child; parents already have this information.

Next, parents can be invited to ask questions. Before the first question, however, request that parents ask one question at a time and that they try to refrain from side discussions. If side discussions begin, the meeting should be halted. Continuing while these discussions are taking place will only add needless confusion to the meeting. Handling such disruptions as delicately as possible, without embarrassing parents, is the sign of a sensitive chair. It is important to respond to questions and criticisms in a forthright and honest manner and to refrain from becoming defensive and angry. The result would be to lose the audience. There is no need, however, to allow the audience to abuse school personnel.

People will get angry, they will become upset, but it is important to keep things moving. Concerns should be addressed as they are raised. Having someone take notes will help reassure parents that school officials are interested in addressing everyone's questions. Repeating what a parent has said can be a positive step for diffusing anger, and it will show parents that school officials are seriously considering what has been said.

Everyone makes mistakes. Admitting a mistake was made and indicating efforts are now underway to rectify the matter works well to diffuse anger. Use caution, however, when making admissions that might leave a person open to legal charges of negligence. Obtaining legal advice before the meeting might be a wise move. In meeting with parents to discuss what occurred and how school officials responded, it is important to avoid becoming defensive and going into long, involved rationales for a course of action. Letting parents know that the school is making changes to insure the safety of the children is sufficient.

Always stress what the school is doing for the children. It is important to reiterate that everyone at the school is working to make sure the school is a safe and happy place.

Ending on a positive note is a key ingredient of a successful meeting. Thanking people for coming to the meeting, for expressing their concerns, for being honest, and for being supportive helps add to a positive atmosphere. At this point it might be helpful to have the school board president, the president of the parish council, or the pastor to stand and say a few words of thanks and express support for all the hard work the school administrators and teachers are putting into getting the school back to normal. School officials may feel awkward about doing so, but they should make this request before the meeting takes place. This supportive statement from someone other than a school administrator is an excellent way of counteracting those people who want to find fault. The end result is that such a statement serves not so much the school officials as the overall best interests of the children.

Summary

This chapter focused on techniques for handling parents during a crisis. The major point was that although many matters may occupy the crisis management team during an emergency, parents must not be forgotten. Failing to respond to parental concerns can result in false rumors, hurt feelings, and a prolongation of the crisis. Suggestions were offered on how to conduct a meeting with parents, with particular attention given to avoiding pitfalls that can extend the crisis school officials are attempting to resolve.

Chapter 10

The Priest/Pastor Responds to Crisis

A n oft-repeated axiom is that people in crisis first turn to their pastor or priest for assistance and support. A critical person in the school's crisis response effort, then, is the parish priest and, by extension, the entire pastoral team. Although the pastoral team may not want to be part of the planning process, sharing plans with them and eventually having the pastor on the crisis management team are vital. This book assumes that faith is that singular dimension that aids an individual dealing with a crisis. Thus, the priest is a key person in conveying the important and correct messages that help bring a crisis to a successful conclusion. This chapter focuses on that role.

Before beginning this discussion, it is important to acknowledge the strained working relationships that often exist between principals and pastors. Most principals assume administrative positions after years of experience as classroom teachers, increased levels of responsibility in a number of schools, and graduate-level studies leading to administrative credentials and degrees. Principals are justifiably hurt and outraged, therefore, when they are confronted by pastors who question the soundness of their judgments and skills in resolving school issues. This chapter is written with an awareness of these strained working relationships.

Pastoral Responsibility

The pastor is mandated to have responsibility for the operation of all the entities that make up a parish, including the parish elementary school and, in some cases, the high school. While he may delegate certain responsibilities to another administrator, the pastor's authority and responsibility are generally quite clear and are well supported in the official law of the Church, the Code of Canon Law. The principal, then, needs to understand the pastor's role within the school and the degree to which the pastor is willing to delegate responsibility.

There is a danger in reading the preceding paragraph from a negative viewpoint. It is intended as a clear, straightforward statement of facts. By understanding their role in parish schools, many principals will understand also the breadth and limits of their responsibilities. Consequently, they will try to avoid situations where polarization occurs and the pastor is placed in the position of having his authority publicly challenged, with the ultimate outcome that the principal has to lose the battle.

Communication

The key word here is communication: work with the pastor to keep open the lines of communication. Often a frustrated principal will complain, quite justifiably, about the pastor's lack of communication. While this may be the case, what is the principal doing to alert the pastor to this problem? Many wise school administrators take on this task as a primary responsibility, with the result that when a major problem does occur, the pastor seeks to confer with the principal before making any public statement.

Working on communication skills means not waiting until a crisis occurs before meeting with the pastor to discuss school concerns. A weekly meeting should be scheduled on the principal's calendar and it can be either part of the pastoral team meeting or an individual meeting with the pastor. If the pastoral team meets weekly, the principal should encourage the pastor to schedule an individual meeting every two to three weeks to discuss matters that may not be relevant to a team meeting or that may be confidential. The principal's goals here are to keep the pastor informed about the general operation of the school and to listen to the pastor's input and concerns about the school.

Crisis Team Formation

In forming a crisis team, the principal needs to discuss all aspects of this move with the pastor and to secure his support. Moving ahead in this critical area without first informing the pastor can be a serious error. When the established crisis team is called upon to function in an emergency, nothing could be worse than the pastor's undermining the team's work because he did not understand how it operates.

Most likely, the pastor will not wish to be a part of the team. If he is to be an ally of the team during a crisis, however, it is important that he be involved either directly or indirectly in team training. It is unrealistic to expect the pastor to show confidence in the team and to support it if he is unfamiliar with its structure and operation. His involvement might entail being kept abreast of developments during the various stages of training or participating in some form of training with the team members. The team could recommend that the pastor participate in one of the simulation exercises contained in Appendix C to help him to understand how the crisis team functions. At any rate, he needs to be kept informed of the team's progress.

Appendix B is an agenda for a team training workshop involving several schools. This model might be useful for training a group of pastors. It could be helpful if a pastor from a school with a successfully established crisis management team serves either as a speaker or a leader of one session. A colleague who has successfully worked with the crisis management team in his parish school serves as an excellent model for other pastors.

A Ministry of Presence

The phrase "a ministry of presence" is particularly appropriate to describe the role a priest or other pastoral representative has when dealing with people in crisis. In hospitals, at the scenes of fires, or wherever people are in crisis, the minister is the one person offering help who has no tools to relieve suffering.

The minister has a different function: his duty is to be present for those who are suffering or grieving over the suffering of others. By being truly present, the minister serves by bringing Christ, or grace, to the particular situation. There is no more beautiful scene than a minister bringing this presence into the midst of chaos and suffering. By contrast, nothing is more tragic than a minister who fails to understand this vital function and seeks to compensate by adopting a different role.

The principal must encourage the pastor and, hopefully, other members of the pastoral team when assisting in a crisis. Being a presence in the midst of an emergency can make the pastoral team a powerful ally to the crisis team's efforts. This is particularly true in situations that involve children who are hysterical and parents who are on the verge of losing control. Assurances from the pastor that the crisis team is working to resolve the crisis are very effective, since his statements of confidence are given great weight by the parish community.

Pastoral Role in a School Crisis

As soon as a crisis occurs, the pastor should be among the first persons notified. Just as the principal would not want to hear about a school crisis from a parent, the pastor would not wish to be blindsided by an upset parishioner. Notification procedures in the manual should detail who notifies the pastor and when he should be contacted.

Even if he has not participated in team training, the pastor may need to be brought in as part of the team during a crisis. He can be effective in reassuring and acting as a good listener to anyone involved in the crisis. His listening can be active in the sense of serving as a conduit between the team and various constituencies, helping team members to understand how others perceive their attempts to resolve the crisis.

The team's ability to define the role the priest should play in an emergency will impact greatly on his effectiveness. A well-trained team will suggest specific actions for the pastor during a crisis. While not attempting to limit his authority or course of action, the team's recommendations to the pastor probably will be received as helpful guidance.

When meetings are held with groups of parents, teachers, or students, the pastor's presence is vitally important, indicating that he is informed and concerned about the crisis. It may be appropriate for him to say a few words of introduction or to make a concluding statement. These brief remarks should always focus on how the team is working to successfully resolve the emergency.

Although some teams may feel it is important to have the pastor seated in a prominent position near the team, thus indicating support for and identification with team members, it is better to have him seated among the general audience so he can watch how the meeting is progressing, observe audience reactions, and later give much-needed feedback to the team.

The pastor may be unwilling to take what he may perceive is a passive role. Indeed, he may feel it is his prerogative to chair such an important meeting. In this case, his wishes should be followed. He may be open, however, to suggestions from the team regarding how he should conduct the meeting. Providing him such assistance in a formal planning session, held a day or two before the meeting with parents, might prove valuable.

Mourning and Celebrating

During and following a crisis, there will be opportunities to gather the school and/or parish community for prayer. These moments of gathering to pray can have a profound impact on everyone, allowing a chance for catharsis and healing. They should become, therefore, part of the crisis team's planning, planning that involves the pastoral team.

Consider asking the pastor or his associates to offer a prayer before any group meetings, in classrooms, in gatherings of the school staff, and when the crisis team begins its work sessions. These prayers may range from an oft-repeated formula prayer to a more structured prayer service. Although prayers and prayer services can be held without the pastor or his associates, pastoral team presence would underscore the importance and meaning of the gathering. Thus, the crisis team may wish to think seriously about asking the priest at those times to be part of its crisis response activity.

At the conclusion of a crisis, or at a burial service, the preference is a liturgical service. In planning properly for this type of gathering, the crisis team should consider how the liturgy can give the individuals gathered a chance to mourn, celebrate, and/or bring some sense of closure to the crisis.

It is important to provide a proper balance in the liturgy between the need to mourn and the need to recognize that life goes on. People need to mourn and express their grief at the profound sense of loss they have experienced. To deny that expression by instituting liturgical practices that deny the reality is to teach mourners, particularly the children, that a sense of loss is not an appropriate feeling. To stifle that expression is to prevent the healing that the community needs so badly.

Repression of reality is especially sad when, during the funeral liturgy of a child, one hears a statement like, "She is better off; she is in a better place." This very subtly discounts the value of a human life and its expression as a gift from God. Rather than focus on expressions that may be inappropriate to the situation, the celebrant should focus on the need for healing and seek avenues for moving that healing forward. This is an ideal situation for which crisis team members may offer to script services that might help the celebrant avoid such pitfalls.

Summary

This chapter examined the important role the pastor plays in a crisis. Beginning with a definition of his role in relationship to the school, the discussion suggested ways in which the priest can provide support and assistance to the team as it works to resolve a crisis. Finally, a brief treatment was presented on the use of prayer and liturgy to help the community begin the healing process following a crisis.

Chapter 11

A Final Word

There are many school projects that call for the principal's attention. Some are fun and exciting, others can be dull and boring, but all are accepted as being part of the administrator's job. Forming a crisis management team is one project that most of us would rather not undertake. No one wants to discuss the possibility of children dying, buildings collapsing, and teachers being traumatized as they try to help children cope with disasters. Yet, if administrators are discharging their responsibilities effectively, they must face the need to consider and plan for all these possibilities.

The preceding chapters presented a systematic plan for developing a crisis response team and handbook for your school. They acknowledged the distinction in organization between public and private schools and presented a plan based on that difference.

Rather than focus on weaknesses in private schools when compared to their public counterparts, this book focused on strengths and how to build positively on them. Recognizing that it is impossible to address all the possible variations in Catholic schools and their differing patterns of organization, the discussion focused on developing a plan for (1) writing a crisis response manual, (2) pulling together and training a crisis response team, and (3) raising the school community's awareness of the need for crisis preparation.

As has been emphasized throughout this book, developing such a plan is not an easy task, but in moving to achieve the goals outlined above, the principal will be working to insure the safety of the lives entrusted to the school's care. This is an awesome responsibility, but if it is taken to heart, then the thankless but essential task of organizing crisis response can begin.

References

Alsalam, N., Ogle, L. T., Rogers, G. T., & Smith, T. M. (1992). *The condition of education, 1992.* Washington, DC: U.S. Department of Education, National Center for Educational Statistics.

Ault, R. L. (1983). *Children's cognitive development* (2nd ed.). New York: Oxford.

Bjorklund, D. F. (1989). *Children's thinking: Developmental function and individual differences.* Pacific Grove, CA: Brooks/Cole.

Harper, S. (1989). *School crisis prevention and response* (NSSC resource paper). Malibu, CA: National School Safety Center.

Kalafat, J. (1990). Adolescent suicide and the implication for school response programs. *School Counselor, 37*(5), 359-369.

Kneisel, P. J., & Richards, G. P. (1988). Crisis intervention after the suicide of a teacher. *Professional Psychology Research and Practice, 19*(2), 165-169.

Leung, B. P. (1993). *School site crisis intervention team handbook.* Unpublished manuscript.

Siehl, P. M. (1990). Suicide postvention: A new disaster plan —What a school should do when faced with a suicide. *School Counselor, 38,* 52-57.

Taylor, R. D., Brady, M. P., & Swank, P. R. (1991). Crisis intervention: Longer-term training effects. *Psychological Reports, 68,* 513-514.

Watson, R. S., Poda, J. H., Miller, C. T., Rice, E. S., & West, G. (1990). *Containing crisis: A guide to managing school emergencies.* Bloomington, IN: National Educational Services.

Youth violence reflects culture. (1993, October). *The Menninger Letter, 1*(10), p. 6.

Appendices

Each of the three appendices contains several items that may be helpful to you in beginning work with the crisis management team and during training.

First there is a suggested outline for the crisis team manual discussed earlier, which may be modified to meet the particular needs of your school.

Second is a suggested agenda for a day-long workshop. In its conceptual form, the workshop probably will work best if conducted with several other schools. Allowing for the cross-fertilization of ideas generally proves beneficial. Furthermore, you will find it much easier to get guest speakers to address the meeting when they know in advance that more than one school is represented.

The last appendix is a set of ten practice simulations that will help the team in its training sessions.

School Crisis Team Response Manual

Suggested Outline

I. Conceptual statement of purpose and scope of responsibilities

II. List of team members, addresses, telephone numbers
   A. Who is notified and in what order
   B. Plan for assumption of responsibility by alternate team leader

III. Description of school site
   A. Drawings of buildings and location of architect's plans
   B. Notes on peculiarities of building sites
   C. List of all shutoff and cutoff points for power
   D. Notes on and location of hazardous areas near school site

IV. Crisis team management center
   A. Description of available resources
   B. Alternate site
   C. Communication plan

V. Evacuation plan for building
   A. List of alternate routes if hallways and doorways are blocked
   B. Area for assembly away from building (away from trees, electrical wires, and autos)

VI. Disaster response plan
   A. General procedure by type of disaster
   B. Assignment of responsibilities
   C. Agencies to contact
   D. Location and general inventory of supplies

VII. Nondisaster-type crises
   A. Description of crises team can handle
   B. Assignment of responsibilities

       C. Resource personnel to contact

       D. Diocesan personnel to contact

VIII. Training

       A. Resource personnel to contact

       B. Plan for team training/needs of team

       C. Plan for staff training

  IX. List of all personnel

       A. Students

          1. Parent-contact information

          2. Students with special needs/problems

       B. Staff

          1. Names, addresses, and telephone numbers

          2. Staff with special needs (e.g., taking special medications)

Team Training Workshop

Suggested Agenda

This sample agenda presumes a school-based team has been formed and that the team has completed several preliminary steps: (a) the school-site survey has been completed, (b) initial work has begun on writing the statements of purpose and overview of the school, and (c) members have discussed and have a basic understanding of their roles as a school-based crisis management team. To maximize the utilization of resources, time, and sharing of ideas, the workshop should be conducted with several other schools, four to six would be ideal, that are at approximately the same level of crisis team formation.

Personnel: Coordinator for the day (someone who can present an overview of crisis team management and keep the groups on track and functioning); a principal who has a team in place and, if possible, has utilized the team in a crisis; and a speaker from one of the public-service agencies (fire, police, disaster preparedness) who can address the teams on a specific aspect of disaster/crisis response.

Suggested Speakers for Session III: Fire department personnel, police official, disaster response coordinator for city/county, paramedic response team member, attorney knowledgeable about legal issues surrounding disaster response, clergy to address spiritual dimension of crisis response, psychologist/clinical social worker from local hospital, director of corporate communications or public-affairs officer from business/industry to discuss dealing with the press/media during a crisis.

Session I—Learning More About Crisis Management
      Welcome
      Introduction/Overview of the Day
      Review of Work on Crisis Manuals

Sharing how other groups approached writing tasks

Community resources identified by groups

Speaker—Principal

Forming a team

What has worked/What has not worked

Crisis handled by team

Question-answer session

Break

Session II—Practicing What We Have Learned

(Suggestion: Mix teams to allow for maximum exchange of ideas. Participants often benefit from working with members from other schools.)

Simulation Overview

All teams assigned same simulation experience

All teams given large sheets of paper to outline plan of action

All teams required to report actions taken and responses to changes in scenarios as they progressed

Simulation Experience

Debriefing of Teams

Lunch

Session III—Professionals in Crisis Response

Speaker—Fire/Police/etc. Personnel

Overview of Emergency Response

How Agencies Would Work with School-based Crisis Team

How Crisis Team Can Prepare for Emergency

Simulation Experience

Brief simulation experience prepared by speaker

Debriefing of Teams (involve the speaker)

Break

Session IV—Putting It All Together

Summary and Evaluation of What We Learned Today

List of Practical Suggestions

Discussion of Possible Future Workshops/Topics

Adjourn

Practice Simulations

Once a crisis management team has been assembled and the school's crisis response manual has been written, the team should receive training that emphasizes lifelike situations. These will probably work best if the team members do not have a lot of warning, the rationale being the less they are able to anticipate the simulated situation, the more they will mimic actual response. It will also be helpful if team members practice these simulations with as much realism as possible; people should not be allowed to stand back and observe and be uninvolved.

Some simulations ask the reader to stop and do some work before moving on to the next section, where new elements are added. It is important, therefore, to follow the instructions, so the impact of the scenario will not be lessened. A debriefing session is needed following each simulation, to provide time for members to ask what they could do better, or change, in an actual event. With one exception, each scenario is written with the principal as the main actor.

Simulation 1
Auto Accident in Front of the School

It is the beginning of the school day and children are arriving for classes. As you stand in the hallway, welcoming children and sipping a cup of coffee, you hear a loud crash coming from the street in front of the school. The sound is so loud that you nearly spill coffee on yourself and the floor. Rushing outside, you are confronted with the following: A car, driven by one of the parents who was dropping children off for classes, went out of control (apparently the gas pedal got stuck) about a half-block away from the school. The car came careening down the street at about 40 to 50 miles an hour and crashed into another car that also was dropping off children in front of the school.

You observe the following: two crashed cars badly smashed up, gasoline flowing from at least one car; smoke of some kind pouring from the engines of the cars; injured children and drivers, in the cars and on the street and sidewalk surrounding the accident; other children, who were not directly involved, traumatized by the scene and running into the school, away from the school, and into the street. The scene is one of chaos.

a. Discuss the steps you will take and the order in which you will take measures to deal with this tragedy.

b. Within minutes of the accident, a television news helicopter is circling the accident scene, broadcasting a live picture over the local channel. Also, news personnel are arriving at the school, requesting to interview you, other school personnel, and students.

c. Later, as you are dealing with this situation, calls come flooding into the school, tying up phone lines and secretarial staff. You need to have an open communication line. How do you deal with this problem?

d. Many parents are arriving at the school because they have heard about the accident. How are you going to handle them?

Simulation 2
Communicable Disease Outbreak

It is midmorning, and you are sitting in your office working on a report that needs to be completed. The secretary calls and says a health department official is on the phone and needs to talk with you immediately. The official's message is rather brief: Two students, who you thought were out with a flu bug, have been diagnosed as active tuberculosis cases and are presently hospitalized. The health department feels that other students in the school, most likely, have been exposed to the disease and may have active cases also. The official says she will be arriving within the hour to discuss how to proceed.

a. What do you do in the meantime?

b. About a week after the initial call, you hear that rumors are circulating among the parents that this would not have happened if it were not for "those foreigners the principal has been enrolling in our school over the past couple of years." There has, in fact, been an increase in an immigrant population in the school.

Simulation 3
Bus Accident During School Outing

For being the top candy-selling group in the school's recent fund-raising drive, one class was rewarded with a day's trip to an amusement park located about 60 miles from school. You have hired a bus from a local school-bus company, distributed the necessary permission slips for parents to sign, and arranged for a couple of other teachers and a couple of volunteer parents to go as chaperons. Feeling that things at school are going quite well and that you have been putting in a lot of time lately on the job, you decide to go with the group and enjoy a day at the amusement park.

It is now late in the afternoon and you plan to have the bus return to the school by 5:30 p.m. The trip has been a huge success and the children have thoroughly enjoyed themselves. No one has gotten lost, and there have been only a few minor problems. As the bus makes its way along an interstate road, about 20 miles from the school, there is a sudden jolt, the bus goes out of control, careens over the side of an embankment, and lands on its side. Injuries are extensive to those on the bus. You are in serious condition and are unable to help in any way with the rescue efforts. In fact, a couple of the students carry you from the bus, and you are now lying on the side of the road.

Meanwhile, a call concerning the accident comes into the school from the police. The vice principal is at the school, along with a small group of parents who arrived early to await the bus's return. The vice principal must take charge of the situation.

Remember, the principal is injured and cannot participate in the crisis management (not until Item c below).

a. As a member of the crisis team, what is the first thing the vice principal does?

b. Within a couple of hours, rumors begin to circulate that several children have died as a result of the accident.

c. It is now two weeks after the accident. No children have died, but several were injured to the extent that they are just now returning to school. The principal is back at school. At this point, rumors are circulating that the accident was due to serious negligence by nearly everyone involved. The rumors say that during lunch, the bus driver, adult chaperons, and the principal were having more than soft drinks with their sandwiches. Several students, so the story goes, told their parents that they saw the adult group consuming alcohol. The rumors, however, are false.

Simulation 4
Sally Dies During History Class

Jim Means, one of your most talented teachers, is holding a lively social studies debate during class. As usual during this teacher's class, students are having a difficult time containing their enthusiasm as the debate over today's topic grows. Hands are going up constantly and students are almost jumping out of their seats to be recognized. Sometimes Mr. Means has to give a gentle warning, "Alright, people, let's take it down a few decibels."

Suddenly a student shouts, "Mr. Means, there's something wrong with Sally." Mr. Means and the rest of the class look over at Sally's desk. Normally a very bright, energetic, and popular student, Sally is now slumped over the desk with her arms hanging limply, obviously comatose. Mr. Means, following school procedure, immediately picks up the intercom phone and alerts the office to the emergency. Paramedics are summoned and they take Sally to the hospital, where she is pronounced dead on arrival.

a. What is the team's immediate response to this tragedy?

b. Students in Sally's class are obviously distraught. What plan do you have for assisting them?

c. Sally's funeral will be held in a couple of days. The family has asked the school to help plan the ceremony.

d. One week later: An autopsy has revealed that Sally died from an overdose of cocaine. The police are at to the school and want to conduct an investigation. They are demanding to interview Sally's classmates immediately.

e. A week and a half after Sally's death: You have received a call from a reporter at the local newspaper who wants to talk about Sally's death and the rumors of "rampant drug use on campus."

f. Two weeks later: Parents are calling to demand that something be done about all the drugs being sold and used at school. You have every reason to believe that Sally's death was an accident. You learned from Sally's parents that her older brother gave her the drug when she complained of feeling "kind of down." He had told Sally it would help her feel better and she was naive and believed him (yes, even bright kids do stupid things!).

g. What long-term plans have you and your team formulated to deal with the effects of Sally's death on her classmates and the school? Do you have any thoughts about Mr. Means and his needs?

Simulation 5
Racial Tensions Erupt on Campus

A point of pride for you and the staff is that over the past five years, you have been successful in making the student population more representative of the racial/ethnic composition of the surrounding community. It has not always been easy, with parent resistance emerging at times as you moved toward increasing the numbers of ethnic minorities. Generally, you have been surprised at how easily the student body has adjusted to this change. Clubs, sports teams, and all levels of instruction are mixed. In fact, you and the staff have not felt the need to institute any human-relations programs or to put any emphasis on the changing composition of the student body. That is, not until today.

During a 20-minute midmorning class break that gives students and staff an opportunity to get a snack and something to drink—a time when there are staff and students in the yard assembly area—two students get into a serious fistfight. It is very acrimonious and bloody, with lots of shouting and name-calling. For the first time that you can remember, racial slurs are slung back and forth between the two combatants, as they are led away to the office. Other students are gathered around, beginning to argue back and forth among themselves. Some shouting occurs, but it is quickly suppressed by the staff and, with the sound of the class warning bell, everyone returns to classes.

You decide this is a matter that requires some attention. Adding to your heightened anxiety about this incident is that the two students involved in the fight say this is not the first time that racial slurs have been thrown back and forth, nor is this the first fight between racially opposite students. A couple of weeks ago, according to them, a fight involving 10 to 20 students occurred at a local park late one night. This is the first you have heard of this or any such incident.

Note: While working on the following questions, do not read ahead until you are satisfied with your response to the question.

a. What is your immediate response to this situation?

During lunch you are in the school cafeteria when a fight involving about 30 students breaks out, again with racial overtones.

b. What is your plan of action once order is restored?

At 1:30 you receive a call from the secretary saying that a news team, reporter and photographer, from a local television station is in the office and wants to interview you about the race riot that occurred during lunch today.

c. What is your plan for dealing with the news media? They insist that whether or not you agree to an interview, they are going to do a live feed in front of the school at 5:00 and admit they have already interviewed several students off campus.

Early the next morning, before the beginning of the school day, you get a call from a student who refuses to identify herself. She says that several students are coming to school armed with weapons. You ask for names, but the student hangs up without giving you any additional information.

d. What is your plan at this point?

It is now several weeks later, and you did discover that a couple of students came to school armed with weapons. You were only able to identify these armed students after another student told a trusted teacher their names. You have been working with the crisis management team and the school staff to institute human-relations training.

e. What is your plan for carrying out human-relations training?

During the time that you have begun to consider human-relations training programs, parents have become increasingly aroused and opposed to your handling of the situation. They blame you for all the trouble that has occurred and the resulting negative publicity.

f. How do you deal with this situation?

Simulation 6
Tim Is Injured at Recess

Ten-year-old Tim, a fourth grader, is enjoying recess with his classmates. He climbs to the top of the jungle gym, which stands approximately eight feet high. Losing his footing and grip at the same time, he slips and falls to the asphalt pavement. He is temporarily knocked unconscious by the fall and blood is flowing from one of his ears. Playground supervisors quickly summon the principal and, because there appears to be a serious head injury and there may be injuries not readily visible, the paramedics are summoned.

a. How do you respond from this point forward? Who do you notify and how do you notify them?

Tim is taken to the hospital, checked over thoroughly, and is soon released to his parents. His parents are directed to keep him home from school the next day and to allow him to return to classes the following day if he feels well enough.

b. Would you change any of your procedures based upon the information you now have?

The night following Tim's injury, parents of his classmates report their children either cannot sleep or, if they do, are experiencing night terrors.

c. How do you respond at this point? Would you change anything in your procedure, or did you make plans up to this point, anticipating this possibility?

Simulation 7
Billy Commits Suicide

Billy Davis is one of the most popular kids in his class. He has been a standout from the first day he entered school. Academically sharp and a gifted athlete, Billy just naturally draws other kids to him. Teachers often note that, although he has a lot of acquaintances, Billy never seems to have any really close friends. Still, he is popular and always seems upbeat, if a bit distant. Lately, teachers are noting that Billy is becoming a bit more withdrawn and quiet. He seems to daydream a lot in class, and has given several of his prized possessions to a couple of his football teammates.

Early Sunday morning you are awakened by a call from one of the parents, informing you that last night Billy drove to an isolated park and shot himself to death. You attempt to contact Billy's parents to offer condolences and any help that may be needed, but a family member tells you the parents are at the police station completing the necessary paperwork. As the day wears on, you think more and more about how you will deal with this situation at school. Late in the evening, the police call to tell you that some kids are gathering at the school and are rather upset over Billy's death.

a. What is your plan of action regarding the kids gathered at school?

b. Do you involve the crisis team at this point? Why or why not?

c. What is your plan for Monday morning?

Soon after the beginning of the school day on Monday, several teachers inform you that everybody in school, it seems, is talking about Billy's death. A lot of rumors are going around, some rather outrageous. Many students are visibly upset and are crying in classes; others are leaving classes and walking around in the building. The football team is gathered in the bleachers, sitting there silently. One of the coaches has decided just to sit nearby, rather than intervene, and is waiting for you to direct how the situation should be handled.

d. How do you move now that the crisis is clearer? Or is it clearer?

It is now a week later. As bizarre as it may seem, two more students, a boy and a girl, have attempted suicide. They were not successful and ended up being hospitalized in the psychiatric unit at the local medical center.

e. Does this in any way affect your plan? Why or why not?

Simulation 8
Crazed Man on Campus

The children are outside for the normal recreation period following lunch. You can hear the usual laughter and yelps that come from several hundred children actively playing at such times. Suddenly you hear something that disturbs you. The laughter has stopped and there is yelling and screaming and the sound of panic. You look out the window to see what is going on, when one of the teachers comes running into your office. You quickly learn that a man who is apparently mentally deranged has entered the school yard, grabbed one of the younger children, and has his hand around her throat as if to strangle her. All the while, he is ranting and raving. Most of the other children have run toward the building and are attempting to enter in a crush of bodies against the doors. A few students are standing on the playground unable to move, frozen in terror.

a. What is your first move?

Within a few minutes, and for unexplained reasons, the man releases the girl he was holding and charges toward the building. You are told that he has entered the building, but his exact whereabouts are unknown.

b. Now what do you do?

A teacher, who had taken her students back to the classroom, hoping that was the safest place, calls on the intercom and gives the coded message indicating that the man is now in her classroom. You determine that he has some sort of weapon and is holding everyone hostage.

c. What is your plan at this point?

The police arrive and the hostage negotiation team talks the man into giving himself up. Neither the children nor the teacher was harmed. In the meantime parents are arriving at the school in droves and are entering the building to locate their children and take them home immediately.

d. How do you handle the situation at this point?

A couple of weeks pass and the school returns to as normal as can be expected given what has occurred. Many parents are still upset, however, and they want a meeting to talk about school security.

e. Do you agree to hold such a meeting? If so, how will you conduct it?

Simulation 9
Natural Disaster

(Depending upon your geographic area, you may want to see this as a tornado or an earthquake. Either will work.)

The school day has begun as usual and soon the sounds that indicate that teachers are teaching, children are learning, and other normal activities of a school day are in progress filter into your office. Around 9:30 you decide to take a tour of the building to make quick visits to a couple of classrooms to observe some teachers.

For the tornado scenario. As you start to leave your office you look out the window and notice that the sky has become very dark. This is not a major concern, just an indication that a storm may be on the way and therefore students will probably not be allowed outside during recess and lunch. You recall hearing some warnings earlier in the morning about possible severe storms in the area. You are still not concerned, because the disaster warning system will alert you to tornado alerts.

As you move around the building, you can feel that the weather is changing. Suddenly, the wind picks up and rain begins to pour. Your first concern is to make sure that all windows and doorways are closed. Before you can begin to check, however, the wind picks up considerably and the building begins to shake, leaving no doubt that the school is right in the path of a major tornado.

For the earthquake scenario. You walk out into the corridor and down the hallway, making your way through the building. As you reach the end of the hallway, you suddenly feel the building begin to shake. At first you wonder if it might be just a heavy truck passing on a nearby street. Then the shaking intensifies, throwing you to the ground, and you quickly realize that the area is being hit by a major earthquake. The shaking lasts for nearly a minute, all the while you hear children screaming, teachers shouting, walls cracking. The ceiling begins to crack and tile falls onto the floor, and you think you hear parts of the roof collapse.

Both scenarios join at this point.

a. What is your first decision?

b. What are your major concerns/priorities?

Major portions of the building have collapsed, several classrooms have caved in, and the gym and cafeteria areas are destroyed.

c. What is your plan of action for dealing with children who have not been injured?

Some children and teachers have been seriously injured but, miraculously, no one has been killed.

d. How will you deal with the injured?

All power and wire communication services have stopped functioning. Streets in the neighboring area are impassable.

e. How does this news affect the way you will handle the situation?

Simulation 10
Food Poisoning During Lunch

You may have to alter this scenario to fit the situation in your school (e.g., if you have no school lunch program, make the scenario involve a problem with the fruit punch or snack served to students as a supplement to their own lunches brought from home).

The lunch period is progressing as usual, with children gathered around tables, eating food, and excitedly talking about their many topics of interest. While most of the teaching staff are having lunch in a room adjacent to the cafeteria, you and some volunteers are monitoring the lunchroom and school yard. You are chatting with one table of students when suddenly you hear a commotion of tumbling chairs and yells from across the room. You look across and see students scrambling to get out of the way of a student who is vomiting on the table and floor. Assuming this is another case of a youngster who, for some vague reason, has become sick during lunch, you walk quickly toward the child while signaling for help to get the mess cleaned up. As you get to where the vomiting student is standing, she suddenly collapses to the floor and, at the same time, two other students become sick and start to vomit.

Still figuring that you have a case of just a few students who have become sick from something they ate, you stick with your plan to take care of the sick students and have the area cleaned up. Within ten minutes, however, you are overwhelmed with calls from throughout the room as additional students complain of feeling ill, are vomiting, and/or begin to faint.

1. How will you begin to deal with the situation at this point?

Because so many children are becoming ill, paramedics have to be summoned (if you have not called for them already). The paramedics assess the situation and suggest the possibility that some form of food poisoning is responsible.

2. How does this information change the manner in which you address the problem?

Some children are sent to the hospital, others are sent home from school, and, finally, the school day ends with over a third of the student body having been involved in the incident.

3. What do you do after school as a follow-up, as it relates to crisis management?

The next day, you receive phone calls and visits from parents questioning the sanitation of the lunchroom and suggesting that the fault lies with food handling by your cafeteria staff.

4. What steps do you take at this point?

Now several days later, the rumors have persisted about poor sanitation and food handling by cafeteria staff. You receive a call from the health department, however, saying that after carefully investigating the incident, they have concluded that it was merely a case of mass hysteria and that there was no real basis in poor food handling to cause the incident.

5. How do you incorporate this information into your handling of the situation?

Although parents accept the cleanliness of food handling by staff, there is a persistent rumor that one or two of the upper-grade boys put something into several students' drinks that caused them to become ill.

6. How do you deal with this information? Do you choose to investigate? Why or why not?

Annotated List of Suggested Readings and Resources

Administrators

Jay, B. (1989). Managing a crisis in the schools—Tips for principals. *NASSP Bulletin, 73*(14), 16-18.
A crisis can happen in any school. Advice, in a case-study format, on what to do when a crisis arises.

Jones, M., & Paterson, L. 1992. *Preventing chaos in times of crisis: A guide for school administrators* (Contract No. 2H86sp03073-02). Rockville, MD: Office for Substance Abuse Prevention. Suggestions to help school administrators develop and implement a systematic crisis response system. Focus is on system organization rather than staff training.

Adoption

Livingston, C. (1990). *Why was I adopted? The facts of adoption with love and illustrations.* New York: Carol Publishing Group.
A real gem of a book for children who are adopted. Deals with the subject and answers questions at a level the child can understand.

Crisis Intervention—General

Colorado State Department of Education. (1990). *Be aware—be prepared. Guidelines for crisis response: Planning for schools/communities.* Denver, CO: Author.
Booklet provides broad guidelines to assist schools and communities in creating individual crisis response plans.

Cultice, W. (1992). Establishing an effective crisis intervention program. *NASSP Bulletin, 76*(543), 68-72.
Outlines a 14-step process for establishing a suicide prevention program.

Feistritzer, P. (Ed.). 1993. Recognizing & responding to at-risk youth [Theme issue]. *Momentum. 24*(2).
Series of articles on many concerns of school personnel dealing with crises.

Glenwick, D. S., Jason, L. A., Copeland, A. P., & Stevens, E. (1979). Crisis intervention in children. *American Psychologist, 34,* 183-185.
Proposes an alternative approach to crisis intervention for community psychologists.

Ingraham, C. (1988). School related crisis. In J. Sandoval (Ed.), *Crisis counseling, intervention, and prevention in the schools* (pp. 35-49). Hillsdale, NJ: Lawrence Erlbaum Associates.
Identifies four common school-related crises and describes students who are at risk of each crisis.

Leung, B. P. (1993). *School site crisis intervention team handbook.* Unpublished manuscript, Loyola Marymount University, School of Education, Los Angeles.
Excellent for developing a crisis team and procedure for response. Dr. Leung is on the faculty of the School of Education, Loyola Marymount University, and would probably respond to a written request for a copy of the manual.

Pruett, H., & Brown, V. (1990, Spring). Present and future issues. *New Directions for Student Services, 49,* 75-81.
Emphasizes the importance of a crisis intervention model that permits a specific staff group with different theoretical orientations to speak a common language.

Roberts, A. R. (Ed.). (1990).*Crisis intervention handbook: Assessment, treatment, and research.* Belmont, CA: Wadsworth.
Describes two detailed crisis management plans developed at Concord (New Hampshire) High School after two tragedies.

Sandoval, J. (Ed.). (1991). *Resources in crisis intervention: School, family and community applications.* Silver Spring, MD: National Association of School Psychologists.
Information to help parents, teachers, and service providers

to plan and implement a comprehensive response to meeting children's emotional needs during a crisis.

Sandoval, J. (Ed.). (1988). *Crisis counseling, intervention, and prevention in the schools.* Hillsdale, NJ: Lawrence Erlbaum Associates.
The first section is on general principles and conceptions of crisis counseling, and the second and third sections discuss particular hazardous events that may result in crises for school children.

Van Ornum, W., & Mordock, J. B. (1986). *Crisis counseling with children and adolescents: A guide for nonprofessional counselors.* New York: Continuum.
For those with no specialized training in child development or counseling, this handbook provides daily applications to a variety of crisis situations.

Crisis Intervention Teams

Guthrie, S. H. (1992). Crisis intervention teaming: A participant's perspective. *School Counselor, 40,* 73-76.
Describes a crisis support plan developed by one county school system to give psychological and physical support to a school facing a crisis.

Purvis, J. R., Porter, R. L., Authement, C. C., & Boren, L. C. (1991). Crisis intervention teams in the schools. *Psychology in the Schools, 28,* 331-339.
Describes steps in establishing a crisis intervention team in schools and presents crisis management scenario.

Death

Bryant, E. H. (1978). Teachers in crisis: A classmate is dying. *Elementary School Journal, 78,* 223-241.
Many helpful suggestions on how a teacher can assist the family and classmates of a dying child to cope.

Garanzini, M. J. (1987). Explaining death to children: The healing process. *Momentum, 18*(4), 30-32.
Offers excellent guidelines to aid parents and teachers working to help a child understand the concept of death.

Mellonie, B., & Ingpen, R. (1983). *Lifetimes: The beautiful way to explain death to children.* New York: Bantam.
Intended for young children, this book explains through words and pictures that all living things go through a life cycle.

Oates, M. D. (1993). *Death in the school community: A handbook for counselors, teachers, and administrators.* Alexandria, VA: American Counseling Association.
Explains in detail how to plan for and respond to deaths that affect a school community.

Sorenson, J. R. (1989). Responding to student or teacher death: Preplanning crisis intervention. *Journal of Counseling and Development, 67,* 426-427.
Describes such a preplanned intervention approach, as successfully implemented in one public school system.

Trachta, A. M. (1988). Postvention: Helping students deal with death. *Psychiatric Hospital, 19*(4), 165-168.
Describes a program developed by a psychiatric hospital to help high school students deal with the precipitous death of a classmate.

Wass, H., Miller, M. D., & Thornton, G. (1990). Death education and grief/suicide intervention in the public schools. *Death Studies, 14,* 253-268.
Survey of 423 public schools on death-related programs.

Divorce

King, M. J., & Goldman, R. K. (1988). Crisis counseling, intervention, and prevention. In J. Sandoval (Ed.), *School Psychology* (pp. 51-71). Hillsdale, NJ: Lawrence Erlbaum Associates.
Describes a spectrum of preventive mental health techniques for marital crises as they affect children and school systems.

Textor, M. R. (Ed.). (1989). *The divorce and divorce therapy handbook.* Northvale, NJ: Jason Aronson.
An overview of contemporary clinical work on divorce and remarriage.

Peer Counseling

Martin, D., Martin, M., & Barrett, C. (1987). A peer counselor crisis intervention training program to help prevent adolescent suicide. *Techniques, 3,* 214-218.

Describes a four-part peer-counseling training program that teaches high school students how to prevent adolescent suicide.

Strip, C., Swassing, R., & Kidder, R. (1991). Female adolescents counseling female adolescents: A first step in emotional crisis intervention. *Roeper Review, 13,* 124-128.

Describes immediate strategic intervention, a counseling strategy that utilizes trained adolescent female friends to help during the first 24 hours of an emotional crisis.

Prevention

Gibson, R. L. (1989). Prevention and the elementary school counselor. *Elementary School Guidance and Counseling, 24*(1), 30-36.

Survey of 96 elementary school counselors on planned prevention activities.

Harper, S. (1989). *School crisis prevention and response* (Contract No. 85-MU-CX-0003). Washington, DC: U.S. Department of Justice.

General preventive school security measures recommended by the National School Safety Center.

Hugill, S., Hindmarch, C., Woolford, A., & Austen, H. (1987). Prevention is better than referral. *Support for Learning, 2*(4), 27-35.

Describes the joint-group work approach between a school and social services for children having social problems at the school.

Suicide

Carter, B. F., & Brooks, A. (1990). Suicide postvention: Crisis or opportunity? *School Counselor, 37,* 378-390.

Describes the clinical process of school-based postvention, which provides assistance to the survivors of a suicide.

Garfinkel, B. D. (1989). The components of school-based suicide prevention. *Residential Treatment for Children and Youth, 7*(1), 97-116.

Discusses suicide prevention programs' focus on such areas as early identification, comprehensive evaluation, crisis intervention, education, and community linkage.

Kalafat, J. (1990). Adolescent suicide and the implication for school response programs. *School Counselor, 37,* 359-369.
Provides an outline and rationale for comprehensive, school-based suicide response programs.

Kneisel, P. J., & Richards, G. P. (1988). Crisis intervention after the suicide of a teacher. *Professional Psychology Research and Practice, 19*(2), 165-169.
Argues that a broad, multifaceted response contributes to the healing process and minimizes mental health difficulties after such an event.

Pruett, H. L. (1990). Crisis intervention and prevention with suicide. *New Directions for Student Services, 49,* 45-55.
Describes a crisis intervention approach that enables the counselor to intervene actively during a suicidal crisis.

Siehl, P. M. (1990). Suicide postvention: A new disaster plan. What a school should do when faced with a suicide. *School Counselor, 38,* 52-57.
Emphasizes the need for school systems to develop planned strategies for dealing with a suicide and presents guidelines to use in developing a postvention plan.

Smaby, M. H., Paterson, T. L., Bergmann, P. E., Bacig, K. Z., & Swearingen, S. (1990). School-based community intervention: The school counselor as lead consultant for suicide prevention and intervention programs. *School Counselor, 37,* 370-377.
Describes a school-based community intervention program led by the school counselor that uses a content consultative approach to create a network between the school and community resources.

7334